Intelligence Surveillance, Security Sector Reforms, Accountability Principles and National Security Challenges within European Union

Intelligence Surveillance, Security Sector Reforms, Accountability Principles and National Security Challenges within European Union

MUSA KHAN JALALZAI

Vij Books India Pvt Ltd

New Delhi (India)

Published by

Vij Books India Pvt Ltd
(Publishers, Distributors & Importers)
2/19, Ansari Road
Delhi – 110 002
Phones: 91-11-43596460, 91-11-47340674
Mobile: 98110 94883
e-mail: contact@vijpublishing.com
www.vijbooks.com

ISBN: 978-81-94285-15-1 (Paperback)

ISBN: 978-81-94285-16-8 (ebook)

Contents

Introduction   1

Chapter 1   Tight-Corner of Intelligence and Surveillance Mechanism within the European Union   15

* Intelligence and Accountability Principles: Dilemma for Legitimacy in Spain and Brazil   20

Yauri Miranda and Jaseff Raziel.

Chapter 2   Britain's Changing Security Perceptions: The Country's National Security Challenges are Amplifying by the Day   24

Chapter 3   Law Enforcement, Security Sector Reforms and the Fight against Radicalization, Drug Trafficking and Terrorism in UK   31

Chapter 4   Bulk Surveillance in the Digital Age: Rethinking the Human Rights Law Approach to the Bulk Monitoring of Communication DATA   38

Daragh Murray and Pete Fussey

Chapter 5   Germany's Intelligence Reform: More Surveillance, Modest Restraints and Inefficient Controls   75

Thorsten Wetzling

Chapter 6   Theorizing Surveillance in the UK
             Crime Control Field   106

             Michael McCahill

Chapter 7   Artificial Intelligence Governance
             and Ethics: Global Perspectives   127

             *Angela Daly, Thilo Hagendorff, Li Hui,
             Monique Mann, Vidushi Marda, Ben Wagner,
             Wei Wang and Saskia Witteborn*

Notes and References   158

Index   197

Introduction

Globalization, digitalization, and artificial intelligence technologies are fundamentally interconnected, while contemporary experts of intelligence surveillance are increasingly dependent on modern satellite and signal technology. Aggrandizement in modern technology and the interconnectedness of our world means that the information environment has manifested phenomenal growth. Over the last two decades, Denmark, France, Germany, Poland, Romania, Netherlands and the United Kingdom proposed different laws, measures and strategies that legalized the powers of interception communications mechanism. In a rapidly changing environment, Intelligence Surveillance developed through different types of technologies, software, strategies and drones operations in Europe and the United Kingdom. There are various forms of surveillance mechanism, including Human Agents, Computer Programs, and Global Positioning Satellite Devices in Vehicles, Cookies, Face-book, YouTube and Apps that diminished our privacy and family life. In yesteryears, way of interception communications dramatically changed and the aggrandizement of new technologies transformed the way individuals communicate with each other.[1]

Barrister Angela Patrick, (Director of Human Rights Policy at JUSTICE) in her paper warned that surveillance fundamentally occurring without the knowledge of individuals being watched: "Surveillance generally occurs without the knowledge of the individual being watched. Only in the limited circumstances when the information is used in a trial or when an authority acknowledges the surveillance will an individual be able to challenge its propriety. In these circumstances, the European Convention on Human Rights places a significant obligation on the State to ensure that surveillance powers are closely drawn, safeguards appropriate and provision made for effective oversight: [it is] unacceptable that the assurance of the enjoyment of a right … could be… removed by the simple fact that the person concerned is kept unaware of its violation."[2]

However, Dr Richard Clayton of Cambridge University explained importance of Internet and computer in his analytical paper. He also noted that government's interference in privacy is of great concern: "Computers connected to the Internet are given a unique "IP address" and data packets are routed towards this IP address, so where there is direct two way communications it cannot be forged. The IP addresses are allocated to ISPs in contiguous blocks, so if it is necessary to determine "who did that?" then public records can be interrogated to determine which ISP was providing Internet service, and they can then consult their records to determine which customer was allocated the particular IP address at the relevant time. That information does not of course indicate whose fingers were on the keyboard, but it will clearly indicate where to look next or whose door to break down".[3]

In a surveillance state, people live in consternation, fear, and struggling to protect their privacy, family life, business secrets and data. The TruePublica report (23 May 2019) has deeply highlighted social and financial affects of the UK surveillance mechanism. The report also noted concern of the European court of Human Rights that the UK government unlawfully obtains data from communications companies and didn't put in place safeguards around how it did it: "Britain is a surveillance state, the worst in the democratic West. In a short period of time, it has amassed a rather sordid history of citizen surveillance– and it continues to be unlawful. Last September's damning judgment of British security operations against its own people saw the European Court of Human Rights (ECHR) rule that the government had unlawfully obtained data from communications companies and didn't put in place safeguards around how it did it. But what does the state really know about us and what about the future? Under Theresa May in the Home Office, the surveillance state became ever more paranoid. It became the most extreme surveillance architecture ever devised in the West–and still is. And it's getting worse. They wanted it all – compromising (naked usually) images of you, your family and friends, what subscriptions you have, sexual orientation and preferences and with whom, earnings, expenditure and on what – places you visit, dates you went there, what you did when you were there".[4]

Report of the TruePublica also noted weaknesses of the UK government to control its own security services for its illegal demonstration by different means: "The state is so out of control its own security services were diverted away from external threats towards us – law-abiding citizens. It was not long ago that MI5 and GCHQ were accused of infecting domestic civilian equipment with viruses so they could turn on TV's and mobile devices at will in people's homes, they recorded conversations and took photos, hacked into iOS, Apple systems and Android equipment, encryption was circumvented even when it was specifically outlawed. Britain's spy agencies worked with the American CIA and created more than 1,000 viruses and other types of malware to gain access to everyday items and either monitor or steal data. It is not known exactly how much information the state has gathered about its people".[5]

However, the Guardian report (13 August 2019) highlighted role of CCTV and the use of Facial Recognition by the UK police to fight prevailing criminal culture effectively. The report also noted the use of Facial Recognition technology by private firms and landlords across the country: "Arguments about surveillance and privacy are usually framed around Big Brother – the overweening state. But the widespread use of facial recognition in private hands suggests a more urgent danger: that not just Big Brother but anyone in the family can watch, and profit from, our faces. The private landlords of the King's Cross development in London are using facial recognition now in their CCTV surveillance. It is not clear whether this is entirely legal, partly because the owners have been reluctant to disclose what it is they're actually doing. This is a development that looks like the worst of all possible worlds. Visual recognition boosted by AI is cheap, widely available and easily programmed – one hobbyist has used it to train his cat flap to open only when his cat was not trying to carry prey into the house–but it is also worryingly inaccurate. Recent trials by police forces in London and south Wales, among other places, have shown a high rate of false positives, and the rate of inaccuracy is much higher with black faces than with white. A technology that cannot in real life discriminate between individuals will only tend to increase the amount of discrimination in society as a whole. It will spread false confidence and real fear".[6]

Big Brother Watch is consecutively running behind government and private agencies-using multifaceted surveillance against civilians. The organization prepared numerous important reports on privacy and human rights of the UK citizens, and still fighting the long war in all forums. In its recent report, (10 July 2019) Big Brother Watch has noted the hearing of the European Court of Human Rights on the UK mass surveillance: "Today, the Grand Chamber of the European Court of Human Rights heard Big Brother Watch & others' case against mass surveillance practices by the UK government. The hearing saw Government lawyers defending bulk surveillance practices and admitting that even the court's confidential emails could be scooped up by UK intelligence agencies. The Government admitted that the purpose of bulk surveillance "is not to search for the communications of identified targets" but to gather mass data and decide "who should be a target". Government lawyers revealed the UK intelligence agencies' purpose for bulk surveillance powers is to search for "unknown unknowns"–a widely-ridiculed phrase used by former US Defense Secretary Donald Rumsfeld to defend the lack of evidence for weapons of mass destruction in Iraq in 2002. The campaign groups argued that this is unlawful, as it cannot be considered necessary or proportionate in a democratic society and "treats everyone as under suspicion". The UK Government also admitted to deploying "automated rules" and "computerized searches" to sift through billions of intercepted calls, texts, emails and internet records".[7]

Notwithstanding these reports and concerns of civil society in the UK and Europe, public remains in dark about their states offensive surveillance powers and capabilities. European research paper, (Surveillance by intelligence services: fundamental rights safeguards and remedies in the EU Volume II: field perspectives and legal update) has documented all the above-cited developments and complications of surveillance technologies within the European Union member states, and noted that legal developments and data protection mechanisms in the project are welcome developments:

"Targeted surveillance–which applies to concrete targets based on some form of individualized suspicion–is regulated in some detail by almost all EU Member States. By contrast, only five Member States currently have detailed legislation on general surveillance of communications. Safeguards do limit the potential for abuse, and these have been strengthened in some Member States – though less so in case of foreign-focused surveillance. Similarly, safeguards are generally weaker–and less transparent–in the context of international intelligence cooperation, suggesting a need for more regulation of such cooperation. Various entities oversee the work of intelligence services across the EU-28, including the judiciary, expert bodies, parliamentary committees and data protection authorities. In a field dominated by secrecy, such oversight is crucial: it helps ensure that intelligence services are held accountable for their actions, and encourages the development of effective internal safeguards within the services. The judiciary and expert bodies are most commonly involved in overseeing surveillance measures. Specialized parliamentary committees generally focus on assessing governmental strategic policies. Member States have set up such committees for this purpose. Data protection authorities have significant powers over intelligence services in seven Member States, but their powers are limited or non-existent in the rest of the EU – mainly due to an exception for national security matters enshrined in data protection law".[8]

In 2008, the UK national security strategy was published to establish principles of internal and external security mechanism, but, unfortunately, it received sharp criticism from research forums and print media across the country. Strategic Defense and Security Reviews (SDSRs), National Security Capabilities Review (NSCR), and National Security council-all interpreted national security mechanism in different ways, but these interpretations couldn't demonstrated as a long-term panacea to the state vulnerability. To fix the broken window, the three competent intelligence agencies (MI6, MI5 and GCHQ) have been struggling to tackle the exponentially growing insecurity, terrorism, extremism, target killings, and foreign espionage across the country, but their involvement in campaign against international terrorism in Middle East, Persian Gulf and Afghanistan further encouraged these elements to dance in cities and towns with impunity.[9]

In February 2019, Government restored stop-and-search powers law to fight criminals and terror suspects in cities and towns, but unfortunately, police have been less visible in streets and relying on technology to provide them with visibility in towns and cities. Since 2005, the policing intelligence collection has been mostly dependent on CCTV, mobile phones, and surveillance technology to deal with threats like foreign espionage and international terrorism, while in EU member states, human intelligence accompanied by a technical approach to national security challenges was of great importance. The May's government proposed changes to improve professionalism and competency of policing intelligence agencies, (National Intelligence Model, Ballistic Intelligence, Special Branch, CID, cyber forces) and counter-espionage programs, but political and bureaucratic stakeholders demonstrated in opposite direction.[10]

Having failed to tackle target killings, drug trafficking, addiction, terrorism and radicalization, law enforcement agencies now shamelessly use Facial Recognition Technology to further smash curtains of privacy, and family life. Facial Recognition Surveillance has been misused in Europe and the UK since years. The use of this Surveillance system by police created controversies but in legal cases police failed to analyze an image respectively. In 2017, police spotlighted more than 4,000 people as suspected terrorists, but half of them were innocent. However, in July 2019, print media reported violation of human rights in Europe's offensive surveillance operations.[11]

Facial recognition cameras scan everyone within range to make biometric maps of their faces – more like fingerprints than photographs. Millions of people in Britain are scanned everyday without their consent. This is a shocking invasion on our privacy. Research shows that when people know they are under surveillance, they behave like schizophrenic people to avoid unjustified suspicion, where they go and who they go with. This hydra also stumbled upon this author for years. I have depressing experience of the UK police Facial Recognition and intelligence-directed surveillance on my house in Hounslow West London. The Facial Recognition has also been proven to discriminate against people of color, meaning they are more likely to be misidentified and stopped, questioned and searched by the police. And police have often chosen to use it in locations with predominantly black, Asian and minority. However, privacy campaigners also warned that the use of Facial Recognition in shopping centers, museums, conference centers, libraries, streets and other private spaces around the UK can alienate citizens from the state. Studies have shown that Facial Recognition Technology is more likely to misidentify people of color, men and women, being stopped incorrectly. Black and Muslims, minority ethnic people could be falsely identified because police have already failed to test how well their systems deal with non-white faces. The ability of Facial Recognition Software to cope with black and ethnic minority faces has proved a key concern for those worried about the technology, who claimed the software was often trained on predominantly white faces. Research data from a police working group revealed that the UK police former head of Facial Recognition knew that skin color was an issue. The UK Home Office also came under pressure not to pursue the use of Facial Recognition Database in the policing of Britain.[12]

Facial Recognition Technology's indiscriminate and large-scale recording, storing and analyzing of our images undermines basic rights. In 2019, the Investigatory Powers Tribunal (IPT) declared that regulations covering access by Britain's GCHQ to emails and phone records intercepted by the US National Security Agency (NSA) breached human rights law. On 08 July 2019, EU Court of Human Rights announced that the UK Bulk Surveillance Powers can be examined soon. In its recent challenge to the 2016

Investigatory Powers Act (IPA), civil rights organization-Liberty argued that government surveillance practices breach human rights law. Facial Recognition isn't the only surveillance technique on the sticky-wicket; there are numerous means the police use to consternate citizens. In 2013, Edward Snowden pointed to the fact that GCHQ were secretly intercepting, processing and sharing the private communications of millions of ordinary people on a daily basis to Foreign Intelligence Services without a clear legal foundation or proper safeguards. In September 2018, European Court of Human Rights ruled that the UK's communication interception regime was unlawful.[13]

In Europe, several intelligence agencies are spying on their own citizens. This way of controlling population in cities and towns generated negative perceptions in print and electronic media against the state designed strategies to control mind and thought of citizens. Relations between Russia and a number of its immediate western neighbors improved, while Poland and the Baltic states see Russia as a historical friend. The case of Kosovo demonstrates that the international community's effectiveness in capacity building of security sector has been less coherent. The exponentially growing power of Russia and its new friendship with some European states, fighting in Middle East, India's economic development, and the ISIS threat in Central Asia, war in Syria, Iraq, and Afghanistan, military developments in China, and the turbulence of North Africa—all these factors point to the fact that the demand for a well-established professional intelligence agency within the EU parameter clearly exists. In my recent research on the capabilities of EU intelligence agencies and their approach to national security and law enforcement, I often pointed to the fact that numerous flaws of operational mechanism within the EU are matter of great concern.[14]

Research scholar, Dr. Gustav Gressel (25 June, 2019) has argued that EU faces numerous challenges, and the threat of hybrid war. He views the future security scenario in various states as murky, and says internal security crisis can be exploited by external adversaries. He also understands that the EU increased vulnerability to hybrid attacks is not a risk inherent in technological progress and globalization, it is matter of choice:

"The EU today provides several opportunities that external adversaries can exploit. Three main factors matter: the changing post-cold war geopolitical environment; technological and legal vulnerabilities inherent in globalization and the common market; and a post-historical zeitgeist still prevalent in Europe that does not accept that subversion, let alone direct military action, is a threat to the European way of life. In the 1990s Europe was largely surrounded by reforming states or infant democracies preoccupied with their own transformation. Now, the continent neighbors' ambitious powers that seek to project both hard and soft power in Europe. Many of them work with anti-system forces in Europe as well. This power projection can have a variety of aims, including that of spreading states' repressive instincts and ideologies to Europe, which may involve silencing, suppressing, or even eliminating dissidents residing there. Such states may also want to control the narrative on their domestic developments through information operations targeting emigrant communities, but also by gaining control of cultural and religious organizations. In Europe, Russia is the best-known actor in these respects, but Turkey and Iran are also active. Saudi Arabia's influence operations concentrate on the US, but some of them are visible in Europe. Another development is the rise of China and the increasing assertiveness of its state apparatus. While Chinese influence operations are less visible than Russian ones, Chinese economic espionage is very active; China sees Europe as a softer target than the US. It concentrates on launching skilled cyber attacks against industries and research facilities, but its programme also encompasses strategic investments in key technology industries."[15]

The EU faces an increasingly an insecure and instable neighborhood and might further face deteriorating security environment and an unprecedented level of threat, while the Brexit has also made the security of the project complex. Germany and France face wide-range of security challenges including the lone wolves attacks and radicalization, which prompted wide-ranging legal and administrative reforms in these two states. In December 2016, Germany, France and Italy proposed a multilateral cooperation in the field of intelligence sharing to counter extremism and radicalization in Europe, and collectively established three competent institutions such as; Berne Group, Europol and the EU Military Staff, but never thought to tackle the crisis of mistrust to make effective the process of intelligence sharing.[16]

Intelligence effectiveness is important in fighting hybrid war. Other investigative forces, such as police and prosecution services, rely heavily on them. Europe lacks a unified understanding of the level and scale of hybrid threats. However, there is remarkably little research on the decline of state secrecy. Social scientists have instead tended to focus on the 'death of privacy', new surveillance technologies and their impact upon ordinary citizens. However, intelligence agencies in some states are outstandingly failing to collect information of high value beneficial for domestic security. Deploying under-trained and inexperienced intelligence officers with limited knowledge of technical tools or key operational skills in Eastern Europe and Baltic states resulted in the collection of inadequate information about major terror group's operational mechanism.[17]

These flaws needed to be addressed by major EU intelligence and security infrastructures in yesteryears, but, unfortunately, due to their mutual distrust, the case has become more complicated. Over the past 20 years, growing national security controversies mostly revolved around the failure of cooperation among the EU member states, which resulted in adversaries and emergence of major extremist organizations that threatened national security of the region. Thus, cooperation among EU intelligence agencies failed to cultivate a strong relationship with policymakers and a close interaction with the civil society. After the London, Madrid, Paris, Munich and Nice attacks, the EU member states were waiting for miracles to bring a ready-made panacea to their pain.[18]

Meanwhile, the issue of whistle blowers has been great concern of intelligence communities across Europe. Disgruntled officers, workers and bureaucrats can anytime leak secret with a single pen drive. There is remarkably little research on the decline of state secrecy. Some analysts view secrecy as a stabilizing element of the state, not least from powerful corporate interests and lobby groups; it can also facilitate a space of exception. The issue of security breach and secrets leak in Britain has been uncontrollably and heedlessly debated on various forms. Leaks of secret meeting on the operational mechanism of Chinese Huawei products, and leaks of the confidential emails of the UK's Ambassador to Washington that criticized President Donald Trump were heartbreaking revelations.[19] In April 2019; credibility of National Security Council was put at spike by some leaks of the meeting on the Chinese Huawei products. 02 May 2019, Shadow Culture Secretary Tom Watson asked Government to make a statement on the National Security Council (NSC) leak.[20]

Mr. Gavin Williamson was removed as Defense Secretary in connection with the breach. The leaks concerned reports that Chinese telecoms giant Huawei would assist in building the UK's new 5G network. This information was leaked to the Daily Telegraph and an inquiry was launched to find the source of the leaks. Responding on behalf of the Government, Minister for Cabinet Office David Lidington told the House: "The unauthorized disclosure of any information from Government is serious and especially so from the National security Council." He went on to say: "The Prime Minister has said that she now considers that this matter has been closed and the Cabinet Secretary does not consider it necessary to refer it to the police."[21]

A former government National Security Adviser warned that leaks from the National Security Council could undermine the willingness of senior civil servants and intelligence officials to speak freely to Ministers about sensitive issues. Sir Mark Lyall Grant said: "This week's leak of details from the committee was extremely unusual". One Minister told the BBC that the NSC was "the holy of holies", with the leaks branded "simply not acceptable". Confidential emails from the UK's Ambassador to Washington that criticized President Donald Trump were also leaked. Sir Kim Darroch's correspondence contained a string of criticisms of Mr. Trump and his administration-describing the White House as "clumsy and inept". Three days after the leak, Sir Kim announced his resignation as British Ambassador to the United States. In a letter to the head of the Foreign Office, Sir Simon McDonald, Sir Kim said he believed it was "impossible" for him to carry on in his current role.[22]

The failure to intercept or identify terrorists before their attacks against civilians, counterterrorism approach of Brussels, Germany and French intelligence agencies remained in question. There were so many hindrances due to which the EU member states couldn't move ahead with a single voice. Speculations that the security assurance of all member states within the EU was mere a hyperbole as complaints of some Eastern European allies about the Brussels attitude raised several questions. Some expert argued that in majority of the 28 EU states, intelligence and policing infrastructure of the cold war era was still in place, which caused many challenges, while some defended recent legal and democratic changes to the intelligence infrastructure in Germany, France and Romania. In fact, intelligence reforms in these three countries are unfinished and the full implementation of security sector reforms face the wrath of private and bureaucratic stakeholders.[23]

In 2017, I authored two books: (1-Fixing the EU Intelligence Crisis and, 2-Securing the Insecure States in Europe and Britain), wrote articles and reports on EU intelligence infrastructure, and underlined the importance of Security Sector Reforms, legal, political and parliamentary oversight. The old intelligence structure of some states, particularly of Eastern European states needed reforms and reorganization in order to make agencies efficient and ambitious. I wrote a paper on Romanian Intelligence, and it's evolving operational mechanism in 2017. I also pointed to the fact that all these weaknesses and flaws in intelligence infrastructures of the EU member states can put in danger their national security and social and political harmony[24]

In Poland, Serbia, Bosnia, Moldova, Ukraine and Kosovo, no intelligence or successful security sector reform package was introduced to make intelligence fit to the fight against terrorism. No doubt, different legal and political entities overseen tactics and operations of intelligence agencies in all EU member states, but the fact of the matter is that in the presence of political and sectarian affiliations in the ranks of agencies, intelligence and law enforcement authorities couldn't convince locus-communes and government. European Union Agency for Fundamental Rights (2017) elucidated the introduction of some intelligence and security sector reforms in some intelligent states:

> "In Netherlands, the new act on the intelligence and security services 2017 assigns the competence to investigate reported wrongdoing to the CTIVD. In the UK, the intelligence agencies operate by law under the authority of the secretary of state. In France, a June 2017 reform changed intelligence coordination within the executive. National Intelligence council has the specific mandate of setting strategies and priorities of the services. It includes the president and the Prime Minister, Ministers, the head of Specialized Service if required by the agenda, and the national intelligence and fight against terrorism coordinator. In Germany, the reform of 2016 did not change the Federal Chancellery's supervising role over the work of the Federal Intelligence Service (BND) or the coordinating role over the work of the Federal Intelligence Service."[25]

These legal and un-coordinative developments left negative impacts on making process of professionalization of intelligence. The consecutive failure of German intelligence agencies to intercept the lone wolves and religiously motivated Muslim extremists before they translated their ferments and resentment into a violent action raised important questions about its national security approach. The lack of predictable security management in the region is the nucleation of debate today. In Moldova and Georgia, security crisis and political fragmentation gave EU more pain. Moldova's support for the EU integration has been weak, while Georgia was also thinking on the same lines because their citizens faced uneven visa regime within the EU member states.[26] In Spain and Brazil, Parliaments are new actors and have the capacity to demand accounts from intelligence leaders. However, the restraining mechanisms of the authority of the executive hampered insofar members of the Parliament lack knowledge to scrutinize the intelligence activity or depend on the very information and discretional power of those agencies to request information and correct the directives of intelligence. In Brazil, only in 2013, the Commission of Intelligence Activity was enacted and constituted as a permanent legislative body.

Musa Khan Jalalzai

London

15 September 2019

Tight-Corner of Intelligence and Surveillance Mechanism within the European Union

In yesteryears, we have accustomed to dozen of terror-related fatalities in several EU member states that brought to light the Achilles-heel of poor and reluctant intelligence sharing on law enforcement level. Notwithstanding the plethora of books, journals and research papers on national security and intelligence cooperation in Europe, there has been an iota research work on interconnectedness and togetherness since 2001.[1] The arrival of jihadist and radicalized elements-belonging to various terrorist and extremist infrastructures of Asia, African and Middle East, and foundation of their terror financing networks across Europe, exacerbated in the pins and needles of security and intelligence experts that these networks can further cause destructiveness and mortality.[2] However, we were witnessed to the fatalities inflicted by terror attacks carried out by these extremist forces in several EU member states in 2015. These and other national security challenges forced European leadership to concentrate on the professionalization of intelligence cooperation and interconnectedness.[3]

Some states introduced security sector reforms, while some were fighting the old communist security infrastructure in their own states; consequently, attempts to bring intelligence and law enforcement agencies under democratic control faced unbreakable challenges. The EU intelligence cooperation and interconnectedness undergone several phases of changing mechanism, including the incorporation of Eastern European communist intelligence and security infrastructure, and the US war on terrorism, where all European intelligence agencies physically exercised their power and expertise in Iraq, Syrian Libya and Afghanistan[4]. Expert of Security and intelligence, Dr. John M. Nomikos in his recent paper floodlighted intelligence cooperation among the EU member states and stressed the need of intelligence sharing: "European intelligence cooperation is the most important weapon in the fight against the new threats in the 28 EU member states...............Even though, effective intelligence cooperation is hard to achieve even at the national level as different services compete for resources and attention from the decisions makers, past terrorist incidents in Europe served as a wake up for the European commission to promote intelligence-sharing and cooperation among EU institutions and Member States"[5].

Intelligence sharing faced many challenges, including working with undemocratic and communist intelligence infrastructure in Eastern European States; such as Romania, Poland, Moldova, Baltic States, Ukraine and Bosnia, where political, bureaucratic and private stakeholders caused irksomeness and apprehension. They didn't want completion of the process of intelligence under democratic control-making alliances to procrastinate security sector reforms as well. For example, Romania is still fighting the old undemocratic security system, and its reform process is screeching-halt.[6] Consequently, lack of reforms and intelligence sharing caused diversification of state-based threats. The threat of bioterrorism, dirty bomb attacks, and use of radioactive gases have put in danger internal security of all member states.[7] After the Paris, Madrid, London, Munich and Nice terrorist attacks, the EU member states responded to these threats poorly with an amateurish mechanism, and never realized that intelligence and security reform was a must to make intelligence professional and well-qualified.

The Europol and Eurojust came under severe criticism. In Britain, after the London Bridge attacks in June 2017, Prime Minister announced counterterrorism measures and powers, and in June 2018, her government published a revised and amended edition of CONTEST Strategy, and Counterterrorism and Border Security Bill[8]. Despite all these security measures, attempts, and changing national security approach, performance of British intelligence and law enforcement agencies remained poor and contradictory. They failed to tackle more than 25,000 jihadists-dancing in streets and towns of the country where they have established criminal networks[9]. Their lack of coordination, and undependable national security approach raised several important questions. Britain's National Security Strategy failed to keep pace with emerging threats from post Brexit security challenges. National Security Strategy also failed to professionally respond to the exponentially growing espionage networks of foreign intelligence agencies, extremism and radicalization.[10] In 2017, government published National Security Capability Review (NCSR) as a "quick refresh" of capabilities, but authorities in one of government committee said it "does not do justice" to the volatile security environment.[11] Moreover, cooperation with EU intelligence agencies failed to cultivate a strong relationship with policymakers and civil society as well. The country's Snoopers Charter Surveillance (SCS) received sharp criticism from political leaders, civil society and electronic media on its bulk interception communication and acquisition.[12]

On 03 June 2018, the Guardian newspaper reported a damning criticism against the British spies that their share of intelligence was obtained under torture-in breach of official guidance. These allegations were found in a letter sent to Foreign Secretary, Boris Johnson by Emily Thornberry and shadow Attorney General Shami Chakrabarti: "The commissioner's most recent report reveals a doubling of cases considered under the Consolidated Guidance, compared with the last three years, and an unprecedented number of acknowledged failures to apply the guidance".[13] The revelation that the US agencies share intelligence may possibly obtained under torture is an embarrassment to the government. In May 2018, government sought mean-culpa to Abdul Hakim Belhaj and Fatima Boudchar, who were taken into custody by CIA with the help of British intelligence. Thornberry and Chakrabarti argued: "With the recent installation of a new CIA Director heavily implicated in the US torture and rendition programme, the UK government must demonstrate that it takes its compliance with the international prohibition on torture seriously".[14]

Democratic Audit (03 October 2018) in its all-inclusive report assessed ways, in which the UK intelligence is scrutinized, to ensure that the agencies were operating on right direction: "The Intelligence and Select Committee (ISC) remains an imperfect and very limited body for the regulation of the large , powerful, and secretive intelligence services. Despite recent reforms which have seen the body becomes a committee of parliament, and with influence over its membership extended to parliament, it is still a body over which the government and Prime Minister exercise an enormous amount of influence".[15]

There were so many hindrances due to which EU intelligence agencies could not establish a better relationship with the British intelligence agencies. The Netherlands, Denmark, Moldova, Ukraine and Baltic States also felt threatened, and their complaints about the weak intelligence sharing were matter of great concern. Amidst all these controversies, complaints, and failures, on 21 January 2015, French Prime Minister Manuel Valls presented a package of security and intelligence reforms, to make professionalize his country agencies. Before the Nice terrorist attacks (14 July 2016), his reform package failed to address security challenges.[16] However, Germany was dancing to the same tango, when its intelligence agencies failed to intercept lone wolves and Muslim extremism. In Moldova and Georgia, security crisis caused more torment, while their support to the EU integration was weak.

However, amidst this controversial intelligence engagement, German intelligence started spying on France, and created clouds surveillance on US and Britain, and British intelligence was spying on Germany that prompted misunderstanding and distrust. On 06 November 2013, BBC reported head of German Parliament's Intelligence Committee called for enquiries into alleged spying committed by British intelligence in Berlin. Consequently, German intelligence were looking at the US and UK agencies with a hostile mood.[17]

The Belgian Foreign Minister once warned that more intelligence on home-grown extremism was needed after the EU intelligence agencies came under heavy criticism when they failed to share high quality intelligence before the Paris attacks. French Home Minister complained that no information about possible attacks was purveyed by the EU agencies. The German intelligence reforms of 2016 didn't change controversial operational mechanism of the Federal Intelligence Service (BND). The consecutive failure of BND to intercept terrorist attacks in Germany raised several important questions.[18] On 16 February 2018, heads of EU Intelligence Chiefs appealed to the EU leaders for continued intelligence sharing after Brexit. In their joint statement, it was insisted on the cooperation among EU member states to professionally respond to the exponentially growing radicalization and extremism.[19]

On 14 May 2018, Mr. Andrew Parker, Chief of MI5 demanded consistent relationship with the EU agencies: "In today's world, we need that shared strength more than ever", he told German counterpart. In a series of papers, British government issued strongest warnings that internal security of the EU can suffer capability gap.[20] On 20 June 2018, the head of GCHQ made an unprecedented intervention in the dispute with Brussels over post-Brexit security by spelling out how British intelligence had saved European lives. Jeremy Fleming, Director of the Surveillance Agency revealed that Britain had supplied information that had helped to break up terrorist plots in four European countries over the past year.[21]

Intelligence cooperation among the EU member states has always been underwhelming due to different stakeholders, bureaucratic attitude and their personal interests. No country wants to share its national secrets on the pretext that terrorist element may possibly retrieve it.[22] Security expert, Bjorn Fagersten (2015) also noted flawed approach of some EU states towards intelligence sharing: "Scholars of international design suggest that when some states contribute more to an institution than others, they will demand more sway over the institution. Other states will grant this control to ensure their participation. Such hierarchical control can reduce the autonomy loss for powerful states and mitigate the risk of free riding and other collective action problems by allowing some states to monitor others. Elements of hierarchy may thus offer net intelligence gain for an organization such as the EU, as long as it empowers actors with high-quality intelligence capabilities. To a large extent, this was the case in the building of INTCEN".[23]

With the Brexit referendum in 2016, and the announcement of Teresa May government to leave the EU project, relations between the EU member states and the UK remained in strain. However, some provoking statements of British leadership caused further distrust. Prime Minister Teresa May issued some harsh statements, and warned that her government would prepare to crash out of the EU if could not negotiate a reasonable exit deal. However, the EU leaders warned that Britain wouldn't be able to have access to the single market.[24]

Intelligence and Accountability Principles: Dilemma for Legitimacy in Spain and Brazil. Yauri Miranda and Jaseff Raziel

How is the relationship between intelligence and accountability in the last years? In different countries, this dilemma has been treated in a different fashion according to four principles: a) Responsibility, in the internal controls and institutional designs to configure the community of intelligence. b) Regulation, in the oversight and control of intelligence by Parliamentary bodies. c) Justice, as in the judicial authorization and control of intelligence activities that affect fundamental rights of citizens (Bovens et al., 2014); and d) Trust, in the participation of citizens in governmental policies or in the closer connection between authority and legitimacy.

This text shows the basic patterns of accountability in those points, as well as the dilemmas and forms to improve the legitimacy of intelligence services in Spain and Brazil. Those places are selected as representative samples of Southern European and Latin American regions in their historical legacies of intelligence experiences after regimes and dictatorships in the late 20th Century (Zegart, 2000; Cepik, 2001; Ugarte, 2002; Numeriano, 2007; Estevez, 2014). The selection is logical and theoretical, as they could enable an analytical generalization for other cases although without statistical generalizations in each region.

In the case of the first principle, responsibility, enabling new administrative and institutional designs to manage and construct the activity intelligence can be considered as forms of internal control. That is, they work as self-restraining mechanisms that Governments and the administration use to control the activity of intelligence, giving pre-eminence either to CNI or to ABIN in each country. The institutional designs were product of several decades of negotiations and political evolution and show that the intelligence services are structurally sui generis public agencies, hierarchically linked to the Executive Branch - who periodically elaborate a national intelligence policy - and are subject to a special regime that regulates their organization and functioning. Thus, the institutional designs also can be considered as attempts to demonstrate that "something is being done" in terms of intelligence. They are the first step that encompass and demonstrate the functions, tasks, principles and rules that guide this activity, in order to reconsider the mandates and the authority given to those institutions, via indirect forms such as election of governments and coalitions that in turn will establish the directives and missions to intelligence.

As this kind of control is a basic and insufficient form of accountability, it is important to consider the Regulatory principle enacted by the role of Parliamentary commissions in each country. Parliaments are new actors and have the capacity to demand accounts from intelligence leaders. However, the restraining mechanisms of the authority of the Executive is hampered insofar members of the Parliament lack knowledge to scrutinize the intelligence activity or depend on the very information and discretional power of those agencies to request information and correct the directives of intelligence. Moreover, most of the Parliament commissions worked in a reactive base, demanding answers after scandals or evident wrongdoings. In the case of Brazil, only in 2013 the Commission of Intelligence Activity was enacted and constituted as a permanent legislative body. Notwithstanding, the Parliament role is an ongoing process of trial and error that could be improved in order to enhance accountability. In that case, members of the parliamentary commissions responsible for financial control should have sufficient human and technological resources to understand the finances of the intelligence services in order to conduct valid scrutiny.

Moreover, they should have sufficient powers and will to change and implement recommendations in the intelligence services. In that sense, representatives of the people should ensure that there are links between external audit bodies so that the results of ex post reviews and audits can be used to support future proposals. Finally, they should prepare public versions of their actions and make periodic reports of their activities. In terms of the principle of Justice, Courts and Judges should have capacity to oversight the interference against fundamental rights, such as privacy, individual autonomy, not interference in communications and personal data. Yet, since intelligence and security reasons are exceptions to those rules, the exceptional character and intromission on those right needs to be regulated.

In Spain, this oversight is conducted by one State Magistrate whereas in Brazil there is no legal control and authorization to carry out those interferences. However, the real practices and interferences of those rights demand a caution approach to regulate intelligence, promoting individual rights and justice as teleological principles that orient their contingent suspension based on intelligence and security grounds, avoiding, thus, a spurious conflict between liberty and security.

The principle of trust remains untouched insofar the civil agency and role of citizens to oversight intelligence needs prospective studies and approaches. Aside of the role of social groups of pressure, independent media, investigative journalism, and scholars, the direct involvement of citizens to constitute commissions of audit and control, as well as to expand the principles of direct democracy and participatory democratic standards are still debatable in a field encompassed by top-down policies. Yet, the incorporation of the latter principle could be a last barrier to be over passed in order to expand the base of legitimacy of the intelligence activity. (*Yauri Miranda and Jaseff Raziel: University of the Basque Country (UPV/ EHU. Research Institute for European and American Studies (www. rieas.gr), 2019.*

Britain's Changing Security Perceptions: The Country's National Security Challenges are Amplifying by the Day

The exponentially growing violence, terror-related incident, and political turmoil, have put internal and external security of Britain at spike. The country's existing security measures and strategies are incapable of combating the hydra of extremism, foreign espionage, international terrorism, and serious organized crime. Drug trafficking, immigration, and containerized illegal trade, and their detrimental impact on industry and market economy created further complexities for policymakers and law enforcement agencies. Exacerbating domestic tensions between communities and the security apparatus has transpired through a range of strategies aimed at countering and reassessing national security threats. CONTEST and other counterterrorism laws have failed to tackle the core issue. The government passed the 2019 Counter-Terrorism and Border Security Act, providing police officers with authorization to stop, question, search, and detain individuals entering the country from abroad. However, a wide range of human trafficking networks both within and outside the U.K. continued to pose significant challenges for British law enforcement agencies.

Britain has been subjected to a series of terrorist attacks in the last two decades. In 2005 and 2009, homegrown extremist groups targeted both government installations and public places in London. In 2013, attacks on mosques in Birmingham generated significant consternation, and in 2014, the Woolwich attack on a

British army soldier casted doubts on the government's credibility and its law enforcement mechanisms. The three attacks of 2017 caused public's lack of confidence in the authorities for a variety of reasons; police failed to disrupt terrorist plots, as the law and order situation deteriorated, as the media criticized the government's lack of a strategic approach to security threats.

Civil wars in Syria, Afghanistan, and Iraq—along with the British military's involvement in those conflicts—contributed to the deterioration of domestic stability. The threat of extremism and terrorism expanded as radicalized elements that had joined the conflicts in the Middle East, the Persian Gulf, and South Asia, returned to the U.K. with new ideas and ways of thinking. Until 2018, there were more than 25,000 registered extremist and radicalized elements representing a range of sectarian groups in British in towns and cities. However, by any reasonable barometer, the level of security of the United Kingdom in 2017 was inauspicious. That year, terrorists carried out three attacks in which several civilians were killed.

British police and intelligence agencies are undoubtedly well-trained and competent, but their ranks have dwindled.[1] Over the past two decades, police have been a less visible presence in the streets, relying on technology to provide them with visibility in towns and cities. Since 2005, intelligence collection has been mostly dependent on CCTV, mobile phones, and surveillance technology to deal with threats like foreign espionage and international terrorism. Conversely, in a majority of EU member states, human intelligence accompanied by a technical approach to national security challenges was of great importance. May's government proposed changes to improve the professionalism and competence of police intelligence (National Intelligence Model, Ballistic Intelligence, Special Branch, CID, cyber forces) and counter-espionage programs, but political and bureaucratic stakeholders resisted every reform package.[2]

The Independent Police Complaints Commission (IPCC) is the only oversight institution designed to improve the competence of the police force, but its efforts went unacknowledged. The commission was established in 2004 to investigate the conduct of police forces.[3] On January 8, 2018, the Independent Police Complains Commission was renamed as the Independent Office for Police Conduct (IOPC).[4] The Policing and Crime Act 2019 also introduced some changes in the system, but these changes were not implemented.[5] The Home Office and the British Parliament's Intelligence and Security Committee (ISC) remain imperfect with limited capacity for maintaining and conducting oversight over a powerful intelligence infrastructure. Recent reforms notwithstanding, the ISC remains a weak body over which the Prime Minister and government exercise their influence. The editors of The U.K.'s Changing Democracy noted some aspects of security sector reforms as they pertain to the ISC and surveillance operations:

> "Choreographed evidence sessions between the committee and the service heads suggest an over-cooperative, too close relationship. So too does the past willingness of the committee to very promptly exonerate the GCHQ pet-bytes the Snowden revelations and the charges of data collection and surveillance exceeding the agencies remit—a clearance that occurred while the revelations were still emerging. Although the ISC criticized the lack of privacy safeguards in the Investigatory Power Bill, it did not secure major changes in the final act. Security Sector Reforms (SSR) is a complex process. Narrowly defined, it can encompass institutions and organizations established to deal with external and internal threats to the security of the state and its citizens. At a minimum, therefore, the security sector includes military and paramilitary forces, the intelligence services, national and local police services, border, customs, and coast guards. However, it is increasingly understood that SSR is broader than these institutions."[6]

British intelligence agencies supported the U.S.-led War on Terror, arresting civilians and handed them over to the CIA and U.S. military for interrogation. There was some degree of public condemnation over this partnership, but neither Parliament nor political parties were in any position to criticize the security services. On 28 June 2018, the UK Parliamentary Intelligence and

Security Committee's torture and rendition report was sharply criticized by human right NGOs: "The report is bound to contain some revelations and criticism about the U.K.'s agencies, but even more worrying is what it won't contain," said Bellah Sankey, Deputy Director of Reprieve. "The committee only saw what the government allowed it to see, being denied access to individual intelligence agents and could only question senior officers who were not directly involved in alleged torture and rendition," Sankey continued.[7]

On 03 June 2018, the Guardian reported: "Britain's spies stand accused of continuing to share intelligence obtained under torture, in breach of official guidance. However, the Daily Mail reported Shadow Attorney General Shami Chakraborti's anger: "The commissioner's most recent report reveals a doubling of cases considered under the Consolidated Guidance, compared with the last three years, and an unprecedented number of acknowledged failures to apply the Guidance."[8] MPs found that British spies had seen detainees being mistreated at least 13 times and were told by prisoners on 25 other occasions that they were being mistreated. On another 128 occasions, they were told of mistreatment by foreign agencies.[9] But despite having knowledge of malpractice, British intelligence agencies continued to supply questions for interrogations. The U.K. maintains a robust surveillance apparatus supporting police and security agencies in maintaining law and order.[10] GCHQ—the British signals intelligence agency—operates TEMPORA, a surveillance system designed to identify foreign threats and a competent tool for combating domestic terrorism and radicalization.[11]

The role of the Interception Communications Commissioner (IoCC) is widely discussed throughout intellectual forums in the U.K. The IoCC's role and oversight mandate was seen as controversial and serving to alienate citizens from the state and government. The commissioner claimed that, under Part-1, Chapter-1 of the Regulation of Investigatory Power Act 2000, its role was to provide independent statutory oversight over the lawful interception of communication, and also asserted that it also investigates complaints.[12] Civil society and intellectual groups didn't agree with this assessment. The functions of the Office of Surveillance Commissioners (OSC) are not so different from that of Intelligence Surveillance Commissioner (ISC). The OSC use human intelligence sources under the Police Act of 1997, as well as under Part-11 and Part-111 of the Regulations of Investigatory Power Act of 2000 (RIPA). These institutions help the state to maintain security and stability as well as provide important information to intelligence agencies. Further expanding the functions of the Intelligence Surveillance Commissioner was the Justice and Security Act of 2013.[13]

The introduction of mass surveillance programs by British and European intelligence services prompted a nationwide debate on the rights of civilians to be protected from illegitimate or warrantless collection, and analysis of their data and metadata.[14] British newspapers and human rights forums published numerous reports, in which experts expressed concerns about the diminishing privacy of citizens. However, the growing concern of citizens about the right of their privacy has also been reported in print and electronic media, but their voice was never heard.

Google, YouTube, Twitter, and Facebook continue to violate the rights of their users. They operate like intelligence agencies, collecting and noting every aspect of a user's interactions and conversations.[15] "Don't Spy on US," a coalition of organizations released a policy paper in September 2014 highlighting surveillance and intelligence operations and their impact on the privacy of citizens in the EU and U.K.: "In summer 2013 it was revealed that GCHQ was routinely intercepting submarine fiber-optic cables containing private communication of millions of British residents (the 'TEMPORA' program). The reported scale of the interception is staggering: each day, GCHQ accesses some 21 pet bytes of data—the equivalent of downloading the entire British Library 192 times."[16] TEMPORA[17] is a surveillance tool used by Government Communication Headquarters (GCHQ). TEMPORA intercepts communications—collecting information from fiber-optic cables.[18] The system is able to access the data of large amounts of internet users, including personal data, regardless of individual suspicion or targeting. Edward Snowden noted in 2016 that TEMPORA maintains two principal components: Mastering the Internet (MTI) and Global Telecoms Exploitation (GTE).[19]

Some intelligence experts argue that GCHQ is more effective at mass-surveillance than the U.S. National Security Agency (NSA) because TEMPORA has access to all telephone and internet communications—including Facebook and email—across Europe.[20] TEMPORA is comprised of different components codenamed POKERFACE and the XKEYSCORE. In a 2016 television interview, Edward Snowden revealed that the NSA and GCHQ were using a new surveillance system called MUSCULAR, one of at least four other similar programs that rely on a trusted second party. The programs together are known as WINDSTOP. According to newspaper reports, over a 30-day period from December 2012 to January 2013, MUSCULAR collected 181 million records, while INCENSER, another WINDSTOP program, collected over 14 billion records over the same period. MUSCULAR can collect information without needing warrants, and also supports the NSA's PINWALE data collection system.[21]

On 01 July 2015, the Investigatory Powers Tribunal (IPT), which investigates complaints of unlawful contact by the UK intelligence agencies, notified Amnesty International that the British government agencies had spied on the organization by intercepting, accessing and storing its communications.[22] The IPT previously identified one of two NGOs which it found had been subjected to unlawful surveillance by the U.K. government as the Egyptian Initiative for Personal Rights (EIPR) when it should have been identified as Amnesty International.[23] The other NGO which was spied on was the Legal Resources Center in South Africa.[24] The Investigatory Powers Tribunal said that until December 2014, GCHQ failed to provide clear enough details of how it shared data collected from mass internet surveillance. It was the IPT's first ruling against an intelligence agency in its fifteen-year history.[25]

The inquiry was prompted by the revelations from information leaked by former CIA contractor Edward Snowden.[26] The committee concluded that there was no bulk surveillance and gave a lengthy defense on it: "We have established that bulk interception cannot be used to search for and examine the communications of an individual in the U.K. unless GCHQ first obtain a specific authorization naming that individual, signed by a secretary of state."[27] At the time, the government was attempting to restore control orders,[28] but the very concept of control orders had already failed.[29] Unless extremist returnees are de-radicalized at the community level, no control order can prevent them from joining the ISIS terrorist network.

Moreover, Britain faces the threat of cyber terrorism.[30] While GCHQ is a top-notch intelligence agency, the U.K. is unable to counter the threat of Chinese or Russian cyber attacks unless it increases the recruitment of young information warriors.[31] Russia maintains strong cyber forces that make use of technology the U.K. doesn't have. The U.K. Cyber Security Strategy (2011) noted cyber threats were coming from other states that seek to conduct espionage to spy on or compromise the British government, military, industrial, and economic assets, as well as monitoring opponents of their own regimes.[32] Moreover, cyber-attacks that cause environmental and financial damage will carry a 14-year prison sentence.[33] Ironically, U.K. authorities have failed to arrest a single cyber-terrorist thus far, while professional hackers continue to establish their networks in the U.K. and target state institutions with impunity.[34] The U.K. faces a new form of intelligence war in which its institutions are attacked from a safe distance.

Law Enforcement, Security Sector Reforms and the Fight against Radicalization, Drug Trafficking and Terrorism in UK

Recent research reports and international think tanks have documented underwhelming performance of state institutions in Britain. Every six months, government announces new security and immigration measures, which is indicative of its frustration and irritation to control the prevailing atmosphere of fear and consternation.[1] The Police Watchdog reports warned that the police is stuck in the past, using outdated methods to deal with modern, organized criminal networks across the country. Notwithstanding their access to modern technology, the police officers lack proper skills, training, and education. In the Rotherham child abuse case, the police Chief admitted failure: "This is a hideous crime. I am deeply embarrassed. I can say with honesty I had no idea of the scale and scope of this." However, Home Affairs Select Committee also criticized former Chief Constable on how his ignorance over these activities was "totally unconvincing".[2] However, growing numbers of terror-related incident in the country prompted some law enforcement and intelligence reforms to design professional strategies in dealing with the issues of law and order management. But these efforts couldn't succeed due to the clash of interests among internal and external stakeholders. In a country without security sector reforms, the surge of racism and discrimination is too painful.[3]

The existing threat from extremism, international terrorism continues to evolve and has done so over the year 2016 in ways that have attracted public attention.[4] Against this backdrop, British National Crime Agency (NCA) carried out several successful operations-broken criminal networks, and established the rule of law where "No Go" areas were being maintained be smugglers and criminal organizations.[5] The performance of police service in Northern Ireland was reviewed by government through different accountability structures including the Police Ombudsman for Northern Ireland Policing Board (PONIPB), but no effective improvement occurred in community policing due to mistrust between the police and communities.

The New Irish Republican Army (NIRA) continues to challenge the authority of the local government, and create fear in community. The New IRA is the restructure of old PIRA that wants to unify Ireland and Northern Ireland. In 2016, Chief of the UK Security Service (MI5), Andrew Parker warned that terrorist threat persisted in Northern Ireland.[6] On 11 March 2015; BBC reported MI5 raised the alert level across Britain for a Northern Irish terrorist attack from "moderate to substantial.[7] Former Home Secretary, Theresa May said the MI5 alert reflected the persisting threat from dissident republican activity.[8] On March 9, 2015, BBC reported the police approach to law enforcement as peculiar, which typically involved waiting until a crime committed and then attempted to tackle it and arrest the criminal.[9]

The performance of the National Crime Agency (NCA) is also underwhelming as the parameters of drug trafficking, human trafficking and fake currency trade has expanded.[10] The issue of institutional corruption still needs to be recognized. In the National Security Strategy (NSS) of 2010, the word corruption has been mentioned only on page 13. However, the Strategic Defense and Security Review (SDSR) 2010, which fleshes out some aspects and the NSS's implementation strategies, don't mention corruption at all. This inconsistent approach in the UK's policymaking process indicates that corruption is not yet seen as relevant to all aspects of national security. This is a serious mistake that directly affects the development of an integrated strategy for reducing the risk of looming security threats.[11]

The government and law enforcement agencies are on the run; the Prime Minister himself is discontented over the intensifying process of radicalization[12], while Home Secretary is confused how to tackle this hydra.[13] The UK's mujahedeen are arriving here from Syria and Iraq one by one with new ideas, a fresh zeal and a brand new mentality.[14] They represented ISIS here and acted on the behalf of a terrorist leader, Abu Bakr al-Baghdadi. This is what Mark Rowley described as a different kind of threat in scale and nature. In view of these developments, government announced new counterterrorism measures, including a range of powers to block suspected UK jihadists from returning home.[15] The Home Office used to seek the cooperation of intelligence agencies to intercept possible terror attacks. Home Secretary warned, "We are in the middle of a generational struggle against a deadly terrorist ideology."[16]

The failure of the Metropolitan police to address pain of communities and control crime has resulted in mistrust between the police and communities. It was widely debated in print and electronic media in the country. The civil society was of the view that million CCTV cameras, the use of facial recognition technology, mass surveillance, and watchdog organizations from skies to the underground failed to deliver positively or show that they were operating in right direction.[17] Sectarian conflict in Northern Ireland received little attention worldwide as violence continues to inflict fatalities on residents of the province. The threat level in the province is revolving based on the operational strategies of both the IRA and government forces. In 2015 and 2016, police in the province recorded 36 shooting incidents, all but half of the number recorded in the yesteryears. In the same period there were 52 bomb blasts incidents, in which hundreds of civilians were killed. Police recovered more than 66 firearms and 4,418 round of ammunition.[18]

On 22 January 2017, Guardian reported a police officer was shot by terrorists in Northern Ireland. On 24 August 2016, a royal marine was arrested over a terrorist plot.[19] A Home Office spokesperson once said that the current terror threat level was severe, which meant that the attacks were highly likely because the exponentially growing terror networks, extremism, jihadism and foreign espionage diseases are spreading across the country, complicating the task of the policing authorities.[20] The crime rate is rising by the day. The police department mostly depended upon drone surveillance and other electronic means in response to the prevailing criminal culture in the country, but the results are underwhelming.[21] On 19 January 2017, Metropolitan Police Commissioner, Sir Bernard Hogan-Howe warned that the latest rise in violent crime across England and Wales was a matter of great concern.[22] Target killing and murder rose to 40 percent. However, children as young as 12, the police said, were running narcotics drugs trade networks between London and their own countries.[23]

Councilors from 19 boroughs once called on Home Secretary to undermine this business, in which big gangs exploit children. In a letter to Home Office, they warned that the crisis is going to worsen. Recent crime figure showed 12 million crimes committed in England and Wales in 2016.[24] The letter stated, "We believe that county Lines has the potential to be the next grooming scandal, following the child sexual exploitation scandals we have seen in Rotherham, Oxford shire and elsewhere in recent years".[25] The future of the UK police operations has, once more, moved to the centre of the political battleground. Previous government weakened it by interfering in its infrastructure, deployment, and appointment and promotion process. During the last 150 years of the establishment of the UK police force (1829) and the establishment of the police complaints board in 1977, no independent oversight was existed in dealing with complaints in the country. Although royal commission on the police that reported in 1962 come about as a result of the widely publicized dismissal of several officers in corruption and fraud cases: "The police a disciplined body, and proper leadership requires that the administration of justice should be in the hands of the chief constable. Any whittling down of this responsibility would weaken the chief constable's command of the force and this again would lead to a loss of moral and confidence".[26]

However, anti-Semitic incidents too reached a high level with record damage to property, abuse and threats. A Jewish NGO recorded more than 1,168 incidents in 2014. The home secretary termed the figure "deeply concerning". Criminal money continues to be channeled through UK banks to terrorists.[27] On 07 August 2019, Britain's most senior counterterrorism expert Neil Basu warned that the police and security service are no longer enough to tackle violent extremism. Moreover, Prime Minister Boris Johnson voiced for more than 10,000 new prison places to tackle terror networks. Terrorist and criminal mafia groups consecutively ordering the purchase of knives and lethal weapons via facebook. On 09 August 2019, the Guardian reported sale of weapons on the Internet. Every day, the threat of terrorism and violent extremism is growing, which makes the police overactive.

Racism has affected law enforcement efforts because this disease reached their ranks as well. In offices, borough councils, streets, towns, trains and buses, minority communities' are being harassed and tortured. The London Borough of Hounslow and some other council harass and mentally torture poor tenants by suspending their housing benefits for months in the pretext that he/she was no longer living on the address they provided to the council. The Hounslow Council housing strategy is causing communities severe pain. The strategy promotes culture of discrimination and nepotism. Poor tenants are not allowed to access Director Housing office for complaints registration.[28] The Outreach officers demonstrate racism and discrimination, and never addressed complaints and housing challenges of elderly tenants. In my E-mail conversation with the outreach officers (Ms. Evans) of the London Borough of Hounslow on the difficulties of elderly citizens who need council's houses, she categorically said the Borough has no house spare in London, while EU citizens were purveyed jobs within the council departments, and houses as well.

The Hounslow Council's draft Housing Strategy 2019-24 clearly elucidates: "Hounslow's Cabinet agreed to the consultation at the Cabinet meeting on 11 June. The draft strategy includes proposals for delivering new homes, meeting housing need, preventing homelessness and providing excellent housing services for our residents over the next four years. Hounslow Council has a statutory duty to produce a Housing Strategy and a Homelessness Strategy. The combining of these two strategies since 2014 has enabled synergies between homeless duties and the wider housing and council service to be achieved. Councilor Steve Curran, Leader of Hounslow Council said: "Our draft housing strategy sets out our ambition for providing high quality housing for our residents, improved mixed communities, and our response to the Homelessness Reduction Act 2017. It is particularly poignant that two years after the Grenfell Tower fire, we are demonstrating how we are responding to changes in policy brought about by that terrible fire and its aftermath and will regenerate our housing estates and improve our housing stock to reflect the highest standards of fire safety for our residents." Notwithstanding all the above mentioned commitments by the Borough authorities, sick and marooned elderly citizens are living in underwhelming circumstances.

In the UK society, there are several ways to view things evolving. Some sociologists view things with scientific glasses while others take an intellectual approach in perceiving the dynamics of social transformation. When one talks about security and terrorism, he comes across many ideas, hypothesis and reports about the government and its agencies' failure in tackling violent extremism and international terrorism.[29] There are thousands of research papers, essays, speeches and lectures available on the websites of think tanks, newspapers, journals and libraries that address the crisis of national security with different approaches, but the lack of professional approach and coordination in these research materials makes causes misunderstanding.[30]

We live in an age of risk mixed insecurities, anxieties about civilities and anti-social behavior.[31] We hope, policing and intelligence forces will respond to all these torments and threats with a professional security approach in maintaining security and law and order.[32] The chapter on social media added to the law enforcement operation in the UK, though strengthen the resolve of the police, but it also need a new approach to counter criminal culture emerged from Face book, YouTube, Twitter and other online sources.[33] Police and its private partners may find them unable to investigate all the above mentioned emerging threatening environment of fear and harassment, but intelligence-led policing can be more effective.[34]

Chapter 4

Bulk Surveillance in the Digital Age: Rethinking the Human Rights Law Approach to the Bulk Monitoring of Communication DATA

Daragh Murray and Pete Fussey

Abstract

The digital age has brought new possibilities and potency to state surveillance activities. Of significance has been the advent of bulk communications data monitoring, which involves the large-scale collection, retention and subsequent analysis of communications data. The scale and invasiveness of these techniques generate key questions regarding their 'necessity' from a human rights law perspective and they are the subject of ongoing human rights-based litigation. This article examines bulk communications data surveillance through the lens of human rights law, undertaking critical examination of both the potential utility of bulk communications surveillance and–drawing on social science analysis–the potential human rights-related harm. It argues that utility and harm calculations can conceal the complex nature of contemporary digital surveillance practices, rendering current approaches to the 'necessity' test problematic. The article argues that (i) the distinction between content and communications data be removed; (ii) analysis of surveillance-related harm must extend beyond privacy implications and incorporate society-wide effects;

and (iii) a more nuanced approach to bulk communications data be developed. Suggestions are provided as to how the 'necessity' of bulk surveillance measures may be evaluated, with an emphasis on understanding the type of activity that may qualify as 'serious crime'.

Keywords: communications data, bulk surveillance, human rights, Snowden, chilling effect

Introduction

The digital age has sparked a fundamental transformation in state surveillance, both in terms of how surveillance is conducted and the types of insight it is intended to facilitate. This transformation is exemplified by the use of bulk communications data techniques,[1] which involve the large-scale collection, retention and subsequent analysis of communications data.[2] These techniques have now become an integral feature of state surveillance. For instance, United Kingdom (UK) intelligence and security services report that the use of bulk communications data is 'essential',[3] and is a key tool in fulfilling their obligation to protect human rights. Others, however, have highlighted the potential for serious human rights concerns,[4] particularly with regard to rights such as the right to privacy, the right to freedom of expression, the right to freedom of assembly and association, and the prohibition of discrimination. While improved intelligence capabilities can unquestionably facilitate the fulfillment of state obligations with regard to the protection of life and public order, interference with the aforementioned rights has the potential to undermine both individual rights and the effective functioning of participatory democracy.[5]

This article examines bulk communications data surveillance through the lens of human rights law, drawing on social science perspectives to further analyze potential harm and impacts. In doing so, the article recognizes limitations in comprehensively addressing all of the component parts of this issue. By nature, and as discussed below, exhaustive analysis of this highly dynamic area is problematic. Indeed, it is precisely these limitations that challenge the applicability of current human rights law tests. In response, the article highlights several core issues to draw out the inherent complexities, and to discuss how bulk communications data surveillance can be understood, approached and addressed, going forward. The article argues that the human rights law approach to bulk communications surveillance should be refined, and proposes key considerations that should be taken into account. The focus is on bulk surveillance practices as they relate to domestic populations. Exclusively externally focused surveillance raises relevant issues, but poses distinct questions, particularly in relation to the impact of any 'chilling effect'. This type of activity is not discussed in this article.[6]

Although this is an issue of global interest, the UK Investigatory Powers Act 2016, and the case law of the European Court of Human Rights (ECtHR) and the Court of Justice of the European Union (CJEU) are used here for illustrative purposes.[7] The Investigatory Powers Act establishes a legal basis for advanced modern surveillance techniques, and so provides an appropriate framework to address the issues under discussion.[8] Equally, the process surrounding the adoption of this Act resulted in the production of a number of reports analyzing bulk techniques, as well as comments by intelligence and security agencies. These provide significant insights. Mass surveillance techniques have also been actively litigated before European courts in recent years, and a number of high profile cases are currently pending. As such, these courts have dealt with the issue at a greater frequency, and in greater detail, than other human rights bodies. To date, the issue of bulk surveillance has not been comprehensively addressed from human rights law perspective, and no specific guidance exists at the international level. This article intends to contribute to emerging understandings of how to approach this issue.

Human rights law typically applies a three-part test to assess the legitimacy of surveillance measures.[9] First, does a legal basis exist under domestic law, and is this legal basis of sufficient quality to protect against arbitrary interference with the rights of individuals? Second, does surveillance pursue a legitimate aim? Third, is the surveillance necessary in a democratic society – that is, does it answer a pressing social need and is it proportionate to the legitimate aim pursued? [10] Evaluating the legal basis, and the quality of this legal basis, is dependent on the specific legal framework applicable in a given jurisdiction, while the uses of surveillance measures by intelligence and security services typically satisfy the legitimate aim test on the basis of protecting national security or public order.[11]

As such, and to examine the specific human rights issues raised by the bulk collection of communications data at a more universal level, this article will focus on the third part of the human rights law test: evaluating the necessity in a democratic society of bulk communications surveillance. This requires an examination of the potential utility,[12] and the potential human rights-related harm, of this practice. To facilitate an understanding of the core issues, this article is organized over four areas of discussion. Section 2 begins by discussing the nature of communications data, and briefly highlighting some relevant human rights law issues. Sections 3 and 4 then engage in an initial discussion of how bulk communications data techniques may be seen through existing formulations of utility and harm.

Section 3 advances the argument that effective assessment of utility is increasingly challenged in its ability to capture the complexity of contemporary digital surveillance practices. In particular, this is because access to specific information demonstrating utility is circumscribed–often legitimately–by national security concerns, while there is also a more general sense of opacity concerning the instrumentality and impact of digitally generated data. This means that an accurate utility assessment is difficult to achieve. Nonetheless, the benefits associated with bulk practices should not be dismissed summarily. Section 4 examines the other side of the equation, drawing on social science analysis of surveillance to indicate the types of direct and indirect harm linked to bulk monitoring. However, as with utility, this section argues that although factors indicating harm do exist, the precise identification of, for example, a chilling effect is difficult to achieve. Ultimately, the challenges associated with examinations of utility and harm raise pressing questions regarding the appropriateness of the human rights law test, as currently applied, and high- light the need for further transparency in relation to claimed utility, and for further consideration of–and research into – the broader types of human rights harm, including at the societal level.

In an effort to resolve this issue, Section 5 argues that any analysis regarding the 'necessity' of bulk communications data surveillance should take into account: (i) the extent of information revealed by communications data; (ii) the extent to which harm associated with retained communications data affects a broad range of rights; (iii) the ease with which communications data can be subject to analysis; and (iv) the utility of bulk communications data to law enforcement and intelligence agencies. On the basis of these factors it is proposed, first, that communications data be regarded as equivalent to content data and, second, that human rights law should adopt a more nuanced approach to the issue of 'mass surveillance'. In order to take advantage of the utility associated with bulk communications data surveillance techniques, while mitigating the full range of associated types of harm, a clearer and stricter understanding of the types of activity to which bulk techniques may be applied is required. This section provides guidance on how the 'necessity' test can be applied in the context of bulk surveillance, and addresses how current broadly conceived notions of 'serious crime' can be revised.

Understanding Communications Data

The term 'communications data' (or 'metadata') refers to all of the information associated with a communication, apart from the actual substance of the communication.[13] A frequently used example suggests that communications data consists of the information on the outside of an envelope, while content data relates to the information contained within the actual letter. However, this analogy does not reflect the true nature or extent of communications data in the current era, or the fact that it can be just as invasive as content data. The widespread integration of technology into everyday life, coupled with increasing digitization, means that individuals produce significant amounts of communications data in the course of a normal day.[14] This information can reveal extensive insights, such as a near comprehensive record of an individual's movements, with whom he or she communicates, how frequently and for how long. Communications data is not restricted to conventional communications such as phone calls, emails, or messaging, but also includes communication between computers and internet browsing histories.[15]

Communications data is deemed particularly useful for the intelligence and security services when combined and aggregated to produce a near comprehensive record of an individual's communications and internet-based activity.[16] Such data is used to find patterns in, or characteristics of, communications that may indicate involvement in a threat to national security or the commission of a crime,[17] or to construct a more generalized 'intelligence picture' of a particular subject. In particular, communications data can be used to uncover the composition of a network, potential hierarchies within that network, and a series of related yet non-obvious relationships. This information can also be used to develop revealing individual profiles.[18]

Advances in the collection, storage, collation and analysis of communications data have trans- formed the extent of detail that can be exposed. As noted by the Advocate General of the CJEU, the use of such data makes it possible to 'create both a faithful and exhaustive map of a large portion of a person's conduct strictly forming part of his private life, or even a complete and accurate picture of his personal identity'.[19] The Special Rapporteur on Freedom of Opinion and Expression similarly noted:[20] When accessed and analyzed, even seemingly innocuous transactional records about communications can collectively create a profile of an individual's private life, including medical conditions, political and religious viewpoints and/or affiliation, interactions and interests, disclosing as much detail as, or even greater detail than would be discernible from the content of communications alone. By combining information about relationships, location, identity and activity, States are able to track the movement of individuals and their activities across a range of different areas, from where they travel to where they study, what they read or whom they interact with.

For intelligence agencies, the benefit of communications data over content-based information may be demonstrated by the following (simplified) example. If a state agent wishes to identify all those individuals who attended a particular protest march, or all those who oppose government policy in relation to a specific issue, they may attempt to do so using content-based information, but this would require considerable resources.[21] However, a cursory search of retained communications data will immediately reveal all those who were at the location of the protest march during the identified time frame, and all those who contacted a particular opposition group (by phone, message, email, or by visiting a website), and will also instantly provide further information such as how frequently this contact occurred. Those individuals who fall into all of the specified categories may then be quickly, indeed almost instantaneously, identified.[22] In addition to revealing information about an individual's political opinion or participation, communications data can also be combined, analyzed and used to infer other highly sensitive personal information, such as an individual's health status, position in a social network, political affiliation, financial situation or sexual orientation.[23]

Bulk communications data surveillance refers to the large-scale collection and retention of communications data–as opposed to the targeted collection of such data[24]–and is today employed by both intelligence and law enforcement agencies.[25] For instance, the UK Investigatory Powers Act allows the Secretary of State to require domestic telecommunications operators to retain communications data for a period of up to 12 months.[26] The retention of communications data may be requested in relation to a broad range of objectives, which include 'the interests of national security', 'for the purpose of preventing or detecting crime or of preventing disorder', and 'for the purpose of assessing or collecting any tax, duty, levy or other imposition, contribution or charge payable to a government department'.[27] As telecommunications operators are the principal providers of internet access, the Act allows for collection of information relating to virtually every individual within the jurisdiction. The retention of bulk communications data, in itself, constitutes an interference with the right to private life[28] and the right to freedom of expression.[29] In order to determine whether this interference is legitimate or results in a violation of human rights law the three-part test developed by the European Court of Human Rights must be applied.[30]

Bulk communications data surveillance and claimed utility

Evaluating the utility of bulk communications data surveillance is a complex task, and two key difficulties must be highlighted. First, information relating to state surveillance activity remains necessarily restricted, and this factor is heightened in the national security context, despite increased transparency and scrutiny in recent years.[31] Second, it is somewhat difficult to identify the specific contribution of bulk communications data surveillance to particular operations. In this regard, and in one of the few authoritative public sources available on these activities, the UK Independent Reviewer of Terrorism Legislation noted:[32]

> Cause and effect in this area are not always straightforward: indeed it will only rarely be possible to attribute a successful outcome solely to the exercise of a particular power. In almost every scenario to which I have been introduced, both in the course of this Review and in several years of reviewing counter-terrorism operations ... [a] mosaic of different information sources is classically involved in identifying a target or threat.

While acknowledging these complexities, the current human rights law approach nonetheless necessitates that efforts be made to identify the particular benefit of this surveillance practice: this examination of utility is essential in determining whether the techniques are 'necessary'. To analyze these issues effectively, we acknowledge a key distinction between the related themes of 'use' and 'utility'. 'Utility' in this sense constitutes a more value-laden assessment of the worth of these distinct and potential 'uses'. As such, the following four areas of discussion first explore attributions of use as expressed by those who operate and oversee these techniques. Here, reports by the UK intelligence and security services,[33] the UK Independent Reviewer of Terrorism

Legislation[34] and others indicate that the use and utility of bulk data communications surveillance relates to, inter alia, (i) mapping of activity and network composition; (ii) pattern identification; (iii) resource efficiencies; and (iv) the ability to 'look into the past'. While implicit in these discussions, the fifth area of discussion engages in more detailed analysis of utility and the claims made for the operational value of these measures.

Mapping of activity and network composition

The collection and retention of bulk communications data allows intelligence and security services to create a map of all – or nearly all – communications activity. This map may be used to determine the composition of a particular organization or network, identify previously unknown persons of interest, develop partial intelligence leads, link anonymous profiles to real world identities, or note changes in communications activity that may be suspicious.

For example, if certain members of a criminal organization are known, examining a map of communications activity will indicate all those users with whom the suspect individuals communicated, and the relationship between them. This can be used to identify the membership of a particular network or group.[35] importantly; this process may flag individuals previously unknown to the security services. Further analysis of these individuals' communications can then be used to infer whether they themselves are suspect. For example:[36]

The security and intelligence agencies' analysis of bulk data uncovered a previously unknown individual in 2014, in contact with a Daesh-affiliated [ISIS] extremist in Syria, who was suspected of involvement in attack planning against the West. As this individual was based overseas, it is very unlikely that any other intelligence capabilities would have discovered him. This form of analysis may also be initiated on the basis of sparse information, as the ability to place even limited information within a near comprehensive communications data set may well indicate other avenues of investigation. In this regard, intelligence leads[37] ... might indicate that a British extremist who travelled to join Dash in Syria in late 2014, whose full name is not yet known, is trying to make contact with a group of known extremists back in a particular region in the UK. The intelligence might indicate that the group potentially has access to firearms, and may be planning an attack.

In such cases, the analysis of data obtained in bulk is frequently the only means of identifying that involved[38] further analysis may also indicate key individuals within a network. For instance, communications patterns may identify a hierarchy among the members, or interlocutors through which a high percentage of communications pass. The ability to examine individual users in the context of all communications activity also facilitates the identification of 'anonymous' users.[39] Individuals may use specific software or practices to hide their identity. However, by placing the communications activity of an anonymous user within the entire pool of communications activity, patterns or overlaps may be identified.

Pattern identification

Bulk communications data can be analyzed to identify suspicious patterns of behaviour. Unlike mapping-related activity, which depends on previously identified information,[40] this form of analysis is more proactive, and is used to generate new intelligence and to reveal (or 'surface') individuals and devices considered to be worthy of further investigation. For instance, it can be used to flag specific users engaged in 'suspicious' patterns of communications activity, such as visiting specific websites, communicating with certain persons, using particular forms of communication, searching for particular terms online, following accounts, or 'liking' posts on social media sites. These individuals may then be prioritized for further investigation. In relation to social media, for example, the UK security and intelligence services state that they:[41] use bulk communications data and bulk personal datasets to gain vital insights into the plans of those plotting against the UK, and to understand the connections between individuals. These capabilities frequently provide one of the only sources of information at the early stages of an investigation.

This pattern analysis may also be used to search for suspect means of communication and applied to cybercrime as well as counter-terrorism operations. In this regard, it is reported:[42] In 2010, an intelligence operation identified a plot which came right from the top of al-Qaida: to send out waves of operatives to Europe to act as sleeper cells and prepare waves of attacks. The intelligence specified unique and distinctive communications methods that would be used by these operatives. GCHQ, in partnership with many other countries, was able to identify operatives by querying bulk data collection for these distinctive patterns. This international effort led, over a period of months, to the arrest of operatives in several European countries at various stages of attack preparation–including one group literally en route to conducting a murderous attack.

Resource deficiencies

Analysis of retained communications data may facilitate more efficient resource utilization by reducing the number of personnel required to conduct physical surveillance, [43] or by discounting potential avenues of investigation. For instance, if UK security services identify a suspected member of the Islamic State, but that individual does not communicate with anyone within the UK, he or she may accordingly be discounted as a threat to the United Kingdom (and perhaps passed on to other intelligence services), thereby freeing up resources to focus on UK-specific threats.[44] This ability to discount potential avenues of investigation can also accelerate investigative processes, thereby 'enabl[ing] the security and intelligence agencies to narrow down likely targets much more quickly, so that they can focus limited investigative resources where it is really needed'.[45] The intelligence and security services state that access to retained communications data facilitates this process, as it removes the need to make individual requests, or a series of such requests:[46] By using bulk communications data, links can be established that would be impossible or significantly slower (potentially taking many days) to discover through a series of individual requests to communications service providers. This can sometimes be the difference between identifying and disrupting a plot, and an attack taking place.

Related communications data: The ability to look into the past

All of these methods of interrogating retained communications data benefit from the ability to look into the past,[47] and several specific benefits may be highlighted. First, in the event of a crime, retained data allows the security services to 'rewind' events, facilitating the identification of suspects and a better understanding of what happened. For instance, if a body is found in waste ground and murder is suspected, analysis of retained data may indicate the presence of individuals at the location where the body was found and enable investigation of their prior activity.[48] Second, retained data allows analysts to 'look back' and immediately identify a suspect's pre-existing network. It is argued that this ability is particularly important in the context of foreign intelligence activities.[49] Third, pattern identification is heavily dependent on accessing retained data.[50] Fourth, access to retained data facilitates speedier investigations, as the data is immediately available in full, and access is not dependent upon targeted requests. For example, the UK intelligence and security services report:[51]

Following a failed terrorist attack in London in 2007, the security and intelligence agencies were able to confirm that the perpetrators were the same as a group who had carried out another attack shortly afterwards. This was achieved in a matter of hours through the analysis of bulk communications data, and was vital in understanding the scale of the threat posed in a fast-moving post-incident investigation, because of the ability to identify connections at speed; it would not have been possible to do this at speed by relying on requests for targeted communications data.

Additionally, it is important to note that a wide range of other agencies claim utility in the retention and analysis of bulk communications data. Indeed, in the United Kingdom, the same legislation that legitimates the use of this data by the intelligence and security services – the 2016 Investigatory Powers Act–has enabled other agencies, not focused on security, to access and retain access to such information.[52]

Examining the utility of bulk communications data surveillance

In terms of the utility of bulk communications data surveillance in practice, recent releases of information and statistics by the UK intelligence and security services report that bulk communications data has:[53]

- 'played a significant part in every major counter terrorism investigation of the last decade, including in each of the seven terrorist attack plots disrupted since November 2014';[54]

- 'been essential to identifying 95% of the cyber-attacks on people and businesses in the UK discovered by the security and intelligence agencies over the last six months' [to 2016];[55]

- 'been used to identify serious criminals seeking to evade detection online, and who cannot be pursued by conventional means, supporting the disruption of over 50 pedophiles in the UK in the last three years';[56]

- been used 'in 95 per cent of serious and organized crime prosecution cases handled by the Crown Prosecution Service Organized Crime Division and has been used in every major Security Service counter-terrorism investigation over the last decade';[57]

- played a significant role in terrorism prosecution: 'The CPS reviewed a snapshot of recent prosecutions for terrorist offences and concluded that in 26 recent cases, of which 17 have concluded with a conviction, 23 could not have been pursued without communications data and in 11 cases the conviction depended on that data'.[58]

Despite these broad claims of utility, it is difficult to examine the specific role and degree of influence played by bulk communications data surveillance, given the limited publicly available information. From a human rights law perspective, the issue is not whether bulk communications data surveillance is useful, but rather whether it is 'strictly necessary in a democratic society', including whether it is 'strictly necessary … for the obtaining of vital intelligence in an individual operation'.[59] Although this test was applied to content and not communications data, it suggests that should the European Court of Human Rights specifically address bulk communications data surveillance, it may examine whether these techniques constitute a 'vital' part of an operation.

The case studies released by the UK intelligence and security services raise a number of questions regarding the useful/vital nature of bulk techniques. For example, the 'Operational Case for Bulk Powers' presents a case study relating to a terrorist attack being planned in Northern Ireland, where it was suspected that the terrorists 'had already obtained explosives for the attack and were escalating their activity'.[60] In this instance, it was reported:[61]

Bulk communications data provided the breakthrough. Through interrogation of the data, the security and intelligence agencies found previously unknown members of the network and were able to increase their coverage of the expanded group. As a result they became aware of a sudden further increase in activity from analysis of the group's communications activity. This led to police action and the recovery of an improvised explosive device.

This example gives rise to questions regarding the 'vital' role played by retained communications data. If a number of the suspected terrorists were known, this indicates that targeted surveillance could have been initiated. This would facilitate the mapping of the network (by monitoring those with whom the known individuals communicate), and the monitoring of the groups' communication patterns (facilitating, for instance, identification of hierarchies), without the need to resort to retained bulk communications data. Similarly, the 'preventing a kidnap' case study relates to a plot by known terrorists to stage a kidnapping.[62] As the terrorists were known, surveillance could feasibly have been initiated with regard to their devices.

A similar analysis may be applied to the drug smuggling ring example provided by the UK police and the Crown Prosecution

Service.[63] While it may be faster to identify 'the bigger players who have taken care to remain in the background'[64] using retained communications data, the same result could be achieved by the initiation of surveillance targeting identified 'minor players'. The 'vital' role played by retained communications data in these operations is difficult to demonstrate.

Ultimately, the case studies presented by the UK intelligence and security services demonstrate the important role played by retained bulk communications data. They do not, however, unequivocally demonstrate that these measures were strictly necessary, or vital to all of the operations in question.[65] Two points may be made. First, in some of the case studies it is not clear that the same outcome could not have been achieved by initiating targeted surveillance of specific individuals, devices, etc. Second, in other cases the benefit appears to be speed and efficiency.

Accordingly, it is possible that a court may not regard bulk communications data techniques as vital and would therefore find them to be incompatible with international human rights law. Such a conclusion, however, risks simplifying a more complex reality. It is difficult to draw a bright line distinction between those intelligence techniques that are merely useful and those that are vital. An approach that fails to take into account these difficulties risks ignoring factors such as the benefit of developing an overall intelligence picture. As highlighted by the UK Independent Reviewer of Counter-Terrorism Legislation, '[c]ause and effect in this area are not always straightforward: ... A mosaic of different information sources is classically involved in identifying a target or threat, developing an understanding of the situation or taking the decision to launch disruptive action'.[66]

In particular, the embeddedness of these practices within intelligence work renders it difficult to conduct a post-operation review to identify which specific components of the operation contributed to a successful outcome. An operation will necessarily draw on myriad available techniques, and it is extremely difficult to know which will be effective in advance. In this context, serious consideration must be given to the experience of the intelligence and security services and their claims that bulk communications data techniques are 'essential'.

Examining the potential harm caused by bulk communications data surveillance

This section draws on social science research and empirical evidence to examine the potential harm associated with bulk collection of communications data, and seeks to progress beyond the well-worn frame of privacy costs. Any survey of surveillance harm is necessarily selective. The purpose here is not to supply a comprehensive inventory of potential impacts resulting from surveillance.[67] Instead, it seeks to focus the discussion on a number of potential impacts resulting from the rapid spread of bulk communications data collection. Claims and counterclaims are common in this contested field of debate.

In order to establish clarity, social science research and empirical evidence are drawn upon to stake a number of core areas in which potential types of harm from surveillance have been identified. Principal among these are (i) chilling effects, and (ii) shifting modes of suspicion, with the latter subdivided into issues of labeling and mental health. In doing so, a series of arguments are developed which gravitate towards two prominent polarities used to assess the permissibility and impact of surveillance practices. Similar to the debates regarding the utility of surveillance, harm arising from surveillance is a highly complex and contested issue. Analysis of these debates further challenges the adequacy of utility-harm oppositions to understand the benefits and impacts of surveillance practices in the digital age.

Chilling effects

In the context of surveillance, a chilling effect is said to arise when individuals refrain from engaging in certain forms of activity because of the perceived consequences if that activity is observed.[68] Any chilling effect immediately brings into play rights such as freedom of expression, freedom of association and freedom of assembly, as it will impact upon the ability of individuals to freely access information, to develop their understanding of specific issues, to engage in communication – or meet – with particular individuals or organizations, and so on. When these rights considerations are addressed at a societal level, it is apparent that a chilling effect can impact upon the effective functioning of a participatory democracy. In short, democracy is dependent upon an informed citizenry, capable of engaging with a diverse range of ideas, and of challenging the status quo. This is the essence of the 'free marketplace of ideas'.[69] It is the possibility that individuals refrain from engaging in activity perceived to be contentious that risks undermining democracy.

Potential chilling effects brought about by surveillance have long been an area of debate and scholarly interest. The origins of such inquiries are unclear but extend at least to the Watergate-era and the analysis by Gregory White and Phillip Zimbardo of what they describe as the psychological breaching of the First Amendment.[70] Participants in a small study were asked about their views on the legal status of marijuana consumption. These views became attenuated in significant ways depending on their likely exposure to law enforcement agencies for 'training purposes'.

For those authors, 'surveillance engenders both anxiety and inhibition',[71] stimulating inhibitions and encouraging those threatened with state surveillance to 'act in ways to deindividuate themselves by increasing their anonymity and guarding their behavior so that they don't seem "out of line"'.[72] While this study is fairly small, simplistic and 'pre-digital'–and thus restricted in its application vis-à-vis understanding more complex unseen and opaque contemporary forms of surveillance –potential chilling effects have remained a prominent area of debate, and are a key focus of human rights law analysis.[73] These ideas have gained importance since Edward Snowden's revelations in 2013. Indeed, given how the right to freedom of expression applies to more than what is merely said, but also covers a range of communications and interactions, a number of recent studies have been quick to link bulk surveillance activities to wide-ranging chilling effects on freedom of expression and association across society.[74]

However, despite such potential impacts of a surveillance-induced chilling effect on individual rights and the functioning of democracy, robust empirically grounded studies of this phenomenon are rare. An exception to these is a survey by the Pew Research Center.[75] In a survey of 475 adults, the research identified how 34 per cent of those aware of surveillance programmes run by the National Security Agency (NSA) had taken one or more measures to conceal their online information, while 25 per cent stated that they had modified how they used technological platforms. Elsewhere, a survey of 520 US authors by PEN America found that many writers were worried about state surveillance and, as a result, engaged in significant levels of self-censorship.[76] According to this survey, large numbers of writers 'reported avoiding writing or speaking about particular subjects that they thought could make them a target of surveillance',[77] with 28 per cent of participants having reduced or avoided social media contact and 24 percent consciously having avoided discussing particular topics via telephone or email. Significantly, 16 percent of participants stated that they had avoided writing or talking about specific topics in respect of which they would feel they were under scrutiny.

Despite the prominence of this theme, and the apparent–albeit limited–empirical support for its existence, identifying chilling effects is far from straightforward and existing studies are afflicted with a range of shortcomings. First is the issue of generalisability. The aforementioned studies have relied on very small sample sizes and (largely) highly specific contexts. These studies cannot claim a more general societal impact and, indeed, the generalisability of studies on chilling effects are influenced by issues of 'ecological validity', where findings from low stakes scenarios in social psychologists' laboratories face difficulties of replication in the more high stakes and messy social world.

Second, problems exist in capturing how intentions are mobilized. For example, successfully identifying a chilling effect rests on measuring a non-event (such as failure to engage in some form of activity). Also important are problems over accurately measuring distinctions between one's intention to express something and the actual likelihood of articulating such thoughts.

Third, surveillance practices operate in a complex social and cultural milieu, making it difficult to isolate surveillance as the sole driver for mediating specific intentions and types of behaviour. Such circumstances make it challenging to identify the precise driver of any chilling effect, whether it be, for example, fear of a hostile reception from a disagreeing audience, fear of a punitive sanction from more remote and invisible state agencies, or something else. Relatedly, chilling effects may be mediated by a range of subjective, social, psychological and ideological beliefs – such as belief in the legitimacy of state surveillance, levels of fear, perceived likelihood of terrorist attack, demographic location, and so on – which makes additionally complex more generalized conclusions that a censored opinion is related solely to state surveillance.

While encountering similar limitations of sample size and potential for generalization, one recent study does provide a more nuanced and detailed analysis of this latter issue of socio-cultural location.[78] Although small (the sample involved 225 self-selecting participants, and was therefore not controlled for non-response bias), key findings reveal the highly focused impacts of chilling effects and their mediation via a range of subjective and social perceptions. Among the results are suggestions that it is an individual's perceived dissonance with majority opinion, rather than exposure to information about online surveillance, that most heavily influences the likelihood of someone expressing an opinion online.

Thus, it is possible to extend this analysis to identify two major, yet related, implications for the consideration of surveillance chill. First, as numerous other empirical studies have pointed out, chilling effects are not generalisable, precisely because they are not felt evenly across social groups.[79] Second, and as a corollary, it is important to recognize that it is the groups holding the fewest resources and social capital required to challenge authority that are most heavily impacted upon by chilling effects. This has particular relevance for any human rights law analysis as it directly relates to the ability to challenge the status quo and thus to the effective functioning of participatory democracy. It directly brings into play rights such as the rights to freedom of expression and to freedom of assembly. Overall, such insights provide a corrective to crude statements that a linear path exists between state surveillance and a generalized chilling of expression. Available evidence challenges the notion that chilling effects hold a uniform and very general coarse-grained impact across the societal range. Instead, a range of variables assert themselves onto the process, attenuating their intensity, form and prevalence.

Concerns over the ambiguity and reach of chilling effects have found expression in the courts and served to weight arguments against acknowledging surveillance harm. Perhaps most well-known among these occurred just a few months before Snowden's revelations, during the 2013 US Supreme Court defense by then NSA chief, James Clapper, against the challenge by Amnesty International USA to surveillance authorized under the US Foreign Intelligence Surveillance Act of 1978 (FISA). Here, and citing the 1972 Laird v Tatum case that '[a]llegations of a subjective "chill" are not an adequate substitute for a claim of specific present objective harm or a threat of specific future harm', the Court stated repeatedly that claims for chilling effects were 'speculative'.[80]

Nevertheless, one of the most robust analyses of chilling effects focuses on internet usage and, coincidentally, covers the period in which the US Supreme Court ruled on the speculative nature of surveillance chill claims. The study focused on access to 48 Wikipedia articles, selected on the basis of alignment with the keywords used by the US Department of Homeland Security to track and monitor social media. It sought to examine variations in related web traffic for the months immediately preceding and following the Snowden revelations in June 2013.[81] Quantifying such activity through advanced statistical modeling techniques, the authors were able to demonstrate a 'large, sudden, and statistically significant drop in the total view counts' for these articles, an 'immediate drop-off of over 30% of overall views'.[82]

This translated into a reduction of 995,085 views and is suggestive of a substantial chilling effect on online searches. Taken together, available evidence suggests that chilling effects can neither be assumed in their totality nor summarily rejected out of hand as unproblematic. Yet, empirical evidence suggests that chilling effects hold complex and variegated forms and assert diverse impacts most acutely felt outside the 'mainstream' – that is, an underlying element in why individuals modify (or 'chill') their behaviour is to bring their activity in line with perceived majority sentiment. This last point is pertinent to the current discussion, given the implications for individual development and democratic participation.

Reconfigured suspicion and surveillance collateral

Often expressed through a familiar trinity of justifications–that no harm is inflicted, individuals are unaware of being observed, and only the smallest fragments of metadata are recorded – digital data collection and analysis are regularly assigned benign labels.[83] Yet it is also possible to argue that the warehousing of data associated with millions of people, almost all of whom are law-abiding and engaged in normal daily life, exerts a profound impact on how suspicion is rendered and administered. Bulk monitoring elevates millions into the realm of the potentially suspicious in a narrowed field of enquiry. In such circumstances, suspicion does not precede data collection – surveillance is not initiated on the basis of 'reasonable suspicion'. Rather, it is generated by analysis of the data itself.

As discussed below, such practices raise important questions over the role of probable cause and reasonable suspicion alongside issues of due process and the presumption of innocence. These questions are not exclusive to the bulk monitoring of digital communications and exist in parallel with debates that accompany other technological forms of security, such as the use of automatic license plate recognition, [84] thermal imaging, [85] digital facial recognition surveillance [86] and surveillance drones.[87] Yet the scope and scale of bulk collection extends far beyond the reach of these other practices, signifying a transformation in the way in which suspicion is characterized.

Of key concern here is the range of activities that may be described as bulk monitoring. While Snowden's exposure of the Government Communications Headquarters' (GCHQ) TEMPORA programme[88] offers a picture of indiscriminate and comprehensive data warehousing, this should not be regarded as an exemplar for all forms of bulk monitoring. Common to surveillance more generally, there are gradations of intensity, with highest concentrations centered on particular populations, typically those at the margins of society. For example, NSA chain analysis is performed by analyzing associations across degrees of separation, or 'hops' in the intelligence vernacular.

While the net is wide, a filtering and triaging process is at play, which necessarily focuses bulk collection activities in highly specific ways. Attention congregates most intensively at particular nodes, communities and networks, elevating specific populations into the realm of the potentially suspicious. Inevitable among these are cohabiters of identity, culture, ethnicity and territory, as well as any activist and advocacy groups that support these populations: a process we may define as 'surveillance collateral'. Overall, any boundary between bulk collection and targeted surveillance becomes blurred in significant ways. This will bring into play a number of human rights considerations relating, for example, to dignity, non-discrimination and equality.

Labeling

Surveillance collateral may intersect with forms of chilling to assert further potential for harm. For more than half a century sociologists of deviance have developed a series of influential theories identifying the complex individual responses to being labeled as an object of suspicion. Like chilling effects, the feeling that one falls into a suspect group is also sufficient to exert an influence. The processes by which this occurs are complex and controversial. They include individuals who internalize the label of suspicion and increasingly act outside the law,[89] and the ways in which ascriptions of suspicion act as a 'master status',[90] defining individuals as suspects above all other potential attributes. Other, more focused, surveillance-related research argues that a series of deeper transactions occur once someone feels he or she is subject to suspicion. Given the asymmetry of power relations among surveyor-surveyed interactions, this includes the communication of clear messages regarding eligibility for social inclusion and citizenship.[91] This will bring into play a number of human rights considerations relating, for example, to dignity, non-discrimination and equality.

Mental Health

Such transactions of suspicion hold further material effects on the observed. For example, recent studies have evidenced deleterious mental health impacts among those living in communities subjected to increased police scrutiny. Moreover, these impacts are not evenly distributed among all inhabitants of targeted neighborhoods. In one study in New York City, which drew on micro-level health data of over 8,000 cases, researchers found that within areas of high police surveillance activity, it is minorities living in areas of high ethno-racial diversity who are likely to experience the most significant impacts on their mental health.[92] Other related research identifies the gender-related impact of such activities, with men likely to experience markedly higher degrees of psychological distress.[93] While these findings focus largely on visible policing strategies in urban areas and the implications of the extended reach of formal corrections and criminal justice into the civil domain,[94] they hold wider resonance.

For example, in the national security context, research into the UK's anti-radicalization 'PREVENT' agenda has consistently identified how those subjected to scrutiny regularly view state agencies similarly in terms of coercive potential.[95] By extension, further corollary effects of heightened suspicion and surveillance may impact on the ability of non-coercive public agencies, such as social work and community-based organizations, to operate effectively in these same communities. These effects raise clear concerns regarding perceived ability to engage in democratic processes.

Summary

Overall, this discussion has focused on the potential for multiple indirect and less visible types of harm brought by bulk collection and analysis of communications data. In addition to prominent arguments over potential chilling effects is the potential for transformations of established constructions and applications of suspicion in it. Most obvious, perhaps, are questions regarding thresholds for reasonableness or probable cause along with the potential circumvention of the presumption of innocence. Such circumstances give rise to questions of whether simply engaging in certain forms of activity or communication, or a tenuous indirect association with someone worthy of suspicion, becomes sufficient to become an object of suspicion.

Importantly, as discussed above, such consequences are focused heavily on marginalized communities, affecting opposition to the status quo. Labels of suspicion may assert further corollary effects, which may condition the availability of life chances and the sustainability of mental health. These factors demonstrate that significant further research into the impact of a chilling effect is required and that consideration of harm must be broadened beyond an exclusive, or near exclusive, privacy focus. Quite simply, an exclusive reliance on privacy is incapable of addressing the totality of the rights implications.

Re-examining the human rights law approach to bulk communications data surveillance

The above discussion demonstrates the complexities involved in assessing potential utilities and harm associated with bulk communications data techniques. Given the significant human rights issues involved–relating not only to the protection of individuals' rights, but also to the effective functioning of democracy itself – this is of serious concern. In particular, this uncertainty and ambiguity make effective assessment of the necessity of bulk communications data surveillance difficult to achieve.[96] In light of the risks posed by ineffective regulation, and mindful of the need to ensure the full spectrum of human rights protection,[97] a new, more nuanced, approach is clearly required.

In determining how human rights law could more effectively respond to bulk communications monitoring, four factors should be taken into account: (i) the extent of information that can be revealed by communications data; (ii) the extent to which harm associated with the retention of communications data affects other rights; (iii) the ease of analyzing communications data; and (iv) the operational utility of bulk collection. Each of these factors is addressed in turn as they provide the basis for the subsequent recommendations.

The extent of information revealed by communications data

As noted above, communications data is not benign. It can be used to reveal highly sensitive personal information, including sensitive health conditions,[98] psychological wellbeing,[99] sexual orientation, relationship status, political affiliation and activist histories.[100] As the former general counsel for the NSA stated, communications data can 'absolutely tell you everything about some- body's life'.[101]

The broad impact of bulk communications data retention on human rights

To date, courts and human rights bodies have focused primarily on the impact of surveillance in the context of the right to privacy. However, a number of other rights may be affected, and the effect on these rights may be particularly severe in the context of bulk communications data surveillance. Relevant rights include, for example, the rights to freedom of expression, association and assembly, and respect for human dignity. Importantly, although it has not addressed the issue in detail, the CJEU has acknowledged that retention of communications data may affect the willingness of individuals to engage the right to freedom of expression.[102]

Notwithstanding the difficulties associated with demonstrating the chilling effect, particular attention must be paid to identifying and understanding its impacts, given the potentially serious consequences for both individuals and society. For example, if individuals are discouraged from engaging in their right to freedom of expression, this risks impairing the fundamental objectives that underpin the right. The right to freedom of expression is regarded as essential for; interalia, individuals' development and the effective functioning of a pluralist democracy. If individuals are deterred from engaging in expression, or if this expression is restricted, then they cannot fully develop their identity or fully participate in the democratic process.

When individuals are concerned that a state may react to certain types of expression, it is more likely that this concern will arise in relation to non-mainstream opinions, such as political expression–that is, expression that may be regarded as opposing the state, the government, or elements of government policy. If this political expression is restricted, then the ability to oppose government policies will be undermined. Existing research indicates that those most vulnerable to a chilling effect are opposition movements, minority groups, and those with fewest resources to challenge the status quo.[103] The effect is such that it may reproduce marginalization and impact upon, or undermine, the basis of a pluralistic democracy–that is, the ability to debate and oppose government policies. This risks a further corollary – erosion of the right to freedom of expression. This line of reasoning may be extended easily to the rights to freedom of association and assembly.

The ability to analyze communications data

Rights interferences caused by the bulk retention of communications data are significantly compounded by the ease with which this data can be analyzed. The ability of state agents to analyze communications data both removes barriers for conducting comprehensive surveillance,[104] and significantly increases the risk – real or perceived–to specific individuals. In a traditional physical surveillance context the resources required of the state to subject all those potentially of interest are simply too great. As noted in Carpenter-five United States:[105] Prior to the digital age, law enforcement might have pursued a suspect for a brief stretch, but doing so 'for any extended period of time was difficult and costly and therefore rarely undertaken' [citing Alito J in US v Jones, 565 US 400, 429]. For that reason, 'society's expectation has been that law enforcement agents and others would not – and indeed, in the main, simply could not – secretly monitor and catalogue every single movement of an individual's car for a very long period' [ibid 430].

Bulk communications data surveillance extends the possibilities for monitoring beyond the movements of a car, to the movements of an individual and, indeed, an identification of the individual's entire pattern of life. The possibility that individuals or groups may be subject to surveillance is therefore dramatically increased if the state can routinely monitor not just one instance of engagement with this political group, but all engagement, and if this information – and any other relevant data – can be accessed instantaneously with little or no resource implications.[106]

It is this ability to monitor and to analyze that makes communications data so useful for intelligence agencies. Indeed, the UK Intelligence and Security Committee noted that 'the primary value to GCHQ of bulk interception was not in reading the actual content of communications, but in the information associated with those communications'[107] This transforms the nature of surveillance. It is no longer the case that the state can subject certain individuals to surveillance and gain relatively limited insights into their activity. Communications data surveillance makes it possible to monitor virtually all activities of all individuals, to discover and evaluate their relationship with others, and to gain profound insights into their lives.

The utility of bulk communications data collection

The previous subsections focused on the potential human rights harm associated with bulk communications data collection. In developing appropriate human rights responses, it is of no less importance to highlight that the activities of the intelligence and security services do contribute to the fulfillment of states' human rights law obligations. In particular, states are subject to a positive obligation to protect rights, such as the individual's right to life and right to property, from threats posed by terrorists or other criminal organizations. Indeed, the failure of states to 'take measures within the scope of their powers which, judged reasonably, might have been expected to avoid'[108] an identified risk will result in a violation of their human rights obligation. This obligation may apply not only in relation to specific threats against identified individuals, 'but also in cases raising the obligation to afford general protection to society'.[109] In this regard, and as discussed briefly above in Section 2, bulk communications data collection can play a significant role in contributing to the fulfillment of a state's human rights obligations. Lack of knowledge with regard to the techniques used, and the ways in which they are used, make this component difficult to engage with from outside. However, utility of bulk communications data techniques should not be lightly dismissed.

That said, in order to ensure effective oversight and regulation, and to maintain public confidence in the state and its security apparatus, it is essential that transparency be prioritized. The professed utility of bulk measures should be more clearly demonstrated, and their necessity–or strict necessity–more clearly addressed. Public disclosure of certain activities may legitimately be restricted on the basis of national security considerations, but transparency should be the rule and secrecy the exception.

Rethinking human rights law considerations in the digital age

This article identifies how bulk communications data surveillance can both contribute to the protection of human rights and result in harm to such rights. Widespread interference with these rights may have implications both at the individual level, affecting individuals' ability to freely develop their identity and opinion, and at the societal level. The societal effect is such that these interferences may fundamentally alter the balance between the state and its citizens, potentially impairing the effective functioning of a pluralistic, participatory democracy.

At the same time, the protection of individuals' rights, and in particular the right to life, is clearly and appropriately a key concern of the state. Efforts to effectively address this potential conflict are compounded by the fact that a precise analysis of utility and harm, and an identification of the specific role played by bulk communications data techniques in a given operation, is exceptionally difficult. In deter- mining how best to move forward, two factors should be considered. First, the current distinction between content and communications data in terms of the level of rights protection should be removed. Second, a more nuanced approach to the regulation of bulk communications data surveillance should be developed.

Removing the (Now Artificial) distinction between contents and communications Data

To date, courts have drawn a distinction between content and communications data, granting con- tent a higher degree of protection. For instance, in Maximillian Schrems v Data Protection Commissioner the CJEU held that 'legislation permitting the public authorities to have access on a generalized basis to the content of electronic communications must be regarded as compromising the essence of the fundamental right to respect for private life'.[110] This may be contrasted with the finding in Digital Rights Ireland in which it was held that the retention of communications data 'is not such as to adversely affect the essence of these rights given that … the directive does not permit the acquisition of knowledge of the content of the electronic communications as such'.[111] This distinction was also made by the UK High Court: 'interception of content is more intrusive than access to communications data'.[112]

However, the distinction between the content of communications and communications data is no longer viable.[113] As discussed above, the insights revealed by communications data, and the ease with which this data may be subject to analysis, indicate that it is wholly appropriate that communications data and the content of communications be granted an equivalent level of protection. Not only are analyses of metadata as intrusive as the examination of content, but the partition between metadata and content is in itself a spurious distinction. Much of the latter can be discerned from the former and their delineation can be achieved only through highly subjective means.

Simply put, there is no meaningful distinction between the sensitivity of information revealed by content and that of communications data. There is increasing recognition as regards the validity of this conclusion. For instance, the Advocate General of the CJEU has stated that 'the risks associated with access to communications data (or 'metadata') may be as great or even greater than those arising from access to the content of communications'.[114] Similarly, and persuasively in this context, statements from various intelligence agencies indicate a prioritization of communications data over content data.[115] At the national level, this may require modification of the existing legal framework in order, for example, to harmonise the rules applicable to the acquisition, retention and management of content data (that is, through lawful interception) and communications data.

Removing the distinction between communications data and content data in terms of the level of human rights protection is a first step towards a more realistic appraisal of surveillance practices. There are indications that the European human rights system is moving in this direction. In Szabo and Vissy, for instance, the European Court of Human Rights stated that the protections established in the Court's case law–which currently focus on content interception–'need to be enhanced'[116] in order to address bulk communications data techniques. More recently, in Big Brother Watch and Others, the Court stated that it was 'not persuaded that the acquisition of related communications data is necessarily less intrusive than the acquisition of content'.[117]

At the domestic level, the US Supreme Court has also moved in this direction, holding in Carpenter that access to communications data – at least in the context of modern surveillance – required a warrant, thereby treating it as equivalent to content interception.[118]

This re-classification of communications data may raise certain challenges to bulk communications data surveillance regimes, and may require a departure from existing case law. In Maximillian Schrems v Data Protection Commissioner the CJEU held that 'legislation permitting the public authorities to have access on a generalized basis to the content of electronic communications must be regarded as compromising the essence of the fundamental right to respect for private life'[119] and, as such, is unequivocally impermissible. In Digital Rights Ireland, a communications data-related case, the Court reached a different conclusion:[120]

[E]ven though the retention of data required by Directive 2006/24 constitutes a particularly serious interference with those rights, it is not such as to adversely affect the essence of those rights given that ... the directive does not permit the acquisition of knowledge of the content of the electronic communications as such. This finding is in keeping with the existing, but inappropriate, distinction between content and communications data. Going forward, this position should be reconsidered. Any legislation permitting access on 'a generalized basis' to communications data must also be regarded as interfering with the essence of the right to privacy, and thus as unequivocally impermissible, in line with Maximillian Schrems. This is entirely appropriate if content and communications data are to be granted the same level of protection vis-à-vis the right to privacy. The question arises, therefore, as to what this means for bulk communications data surveillance regimes. Key in this regard is the Court's prohibition of access on a 'generalized basis', that is:[121]

> [W]ithout any differentiation, limitation or exception being made in the light of the objective pursued and without an objective criterion being laid down by which to determine the limits of the access of the public authorities to the data, and of its subsequent use, for purposes which are specific, strictly restricted and capable of justifying the interference which both access to that data and its use entail. This does not indicate that all bulk communications surveillance is unlawful. Rather, the legality of any bulk communications data surveillance regime will depend not only on satisfying the necessity test, but also on ensuring appropriate limitations vis-à-vis collection, access, use, sharing, detention, and so on. In Big Brother Watch and Others the CJEU made significant steps forward in relation to safeguards,[122] although these were applied exclusively in

the content of externally focused surveillance activities. These appear to constitute an appropriate starting point, and so attention will now turn to how 'necessity' is evaluated.

Developing a more nuanced approach to bulk communications data techniques: Understanding what constitutes serious crime

As noted, the opacity associated with effectively measuring both the utility and harm of bulk powers renders a straightforward application of the current human rights law test problematic. To overcome these difficulties, it is suggested that a more nuanced approach is required, so that the weakness of this dichotomy and the complexity and dynamism of the operating environment can be fully taken into account. As it currently stands, there is insufficient information in the public domain to take a position as to whether particular bulk powers satisfy the relevant human rights law test and can therefore be lawfully deployed. However, these are live issues – both in terms of legislative developments and judicial proceedings – and so it is essential that the human rights law test be clearly set out. In developing any approach, recourse must be had to existing case law. The required standard was set forth most clearly by the European Court of Human Rights in Szabo and Vissy:[123]

> A measure of secret surveillance can be found as being in compliance with the Convention only if it is strictly necessary, as a general consideration, for the [sic] safeguarding the democratic institutions and, moreover, if it is strictly necessary, as a particular consideration, for the obtaining of vital intelligence in an individual operation. Two core requirements emerge from this ruling. First, the use of bulk techniques must be restricted to circumstances that are strictly necessary to safeguard the democratic institutions. This indicates that powers may be used only in relation to certain categories of serious crime,[124] although this requirement should perhaps be more appropriately read as safeguarding the components essential for a democratic society. Second, if such powers are appropriate as a general consideration, then the strict necessity

test further requires that at an operational level powers must be 'vital' to an individual operation. These requirements will be discussed in turn.

In relation to the first component, it is appropriate that the use of bulk powers be restricted to only the most significant threats. As discussed above, although the harm associated with bulk surveillance is difficult to quantify, it is of a nature to undermine the effective functioning of a democratic society. It stands to reason, therefore, that only threats that themselves threaten a democratic society could justify such measures. However, uncertainty exists as to what crimes may be defined as 'serious' for these purposes. For instance, the CJEU has referred to threats to national security and activities that will affect the monetary stability of the state,[125] while the UK Investigatory Powers Act defines serious crime as that which will result in a three-year or longer custodial sentence.[126] This is a significant difference and clarity is required.[127]

Clearly, defining the specific crimes to which bulk communications data techniques may be applied is an important step. Such a decision should be based upon determining those crimes that constitute a genuine threat to democratic institutions, for which extensive powers are warranted. It should not be based on a general understanding of what constitutes 'serious' crime. Although it is difficult to define 'serious' in the abstract, the human rights law test and the invasiveness of the measures in question point to a high threshold. At issue, therefore, is crime that is defined as actively threatening the functioning of a democratic society –for instance, through attacks on or interference with democratic institutions and processes–and crime that affects the functioning of society itself, for instance through large-scale interference with the ability to live a normal life.

In this regard, serious threats to national infrastructure (such as dams, power plants, or the national grid), serious threats posed by organized terrorism (such as that previously posed by the Provisional IRA) or foreign espionage may satisfy the threshold. Other activities that threaten national security should also be addressed. However, caution is required in this regard, as national security is a broad concept and one that has been abused in the past. Rather than being regarded as a catch-all category justifying bulk powers, only those specific national security threats rising to the threshold elaborated above should be considered. This raises difficult questions. For instance, should the threat posed by lone-wolf attackers are distinguished from the threat posed by more organized terrorist groups?

Equally, the human rights law threshold means that other crimes, although 'serious' in terms of their gravity and impact on affected individuals, will not satisfy the required threshold. For instance, murder is unquestionably a serious crime that will result in a significant custodial sentence. However, it is not of a nature to threaten the functioning of a democratic society. To reiterate, this does not suggest that those crimes that fall below the initial strict necessity threshold are not grave, or do not warrant full and effective investigation. Indeed, in a large number of instances international human rights law requires that effective investigations be undertaken, and requires that the state be held to account should it fail to do so. Rather, it is a clear acknowledgement that bulk powers are particularly invasive and pose risks of harm that may undermine or impair the functioning of a democratic society. Only threats to a democratic society itself can justify such measures.

The second component requires that measures be 'vital' to a specific operation. In the context of bulk powers this is a potentially difficult test to apply as a 'mosaic' of different approaches are used in the development of intelligence or investigative profiles. Care should therefore be taken to develop an appropriately nuanced approach. It may be impossible to make a bright line distinction as to whether bulk techniques are useful or vital in specific operations. However, utility exists across a spectrum, and the nature of the role that bulk powers play may be evaluated in light of the existence of alternative techniques.

Essentially, this requires determining whether other (non-bulk) techniques exist, and distinguishing between those situations in which bulk powers are useful and those situations in which they are 'vital', in that the operation cannot proceed without bulk powers. For example, traditional or targeted techniques are arguably sufficient for murder investigations or efforts to uncover hierarchies within domestic terrorist, drug or organized crime groups. In these cases, although bulk techniques may be useful, proven alternative techniques exist and may be deployed. Of course, important questions do arise in relation to efficiencies generated by bulk surveillance, particularly in relation to time and costs. However, the relevance of these factors must be considered in light of the invasiveness of the techniques and it does not seem appropriate that they should be decisive for those crimes falling below the 'serious crime' threshold.

Bulk techniques may play a far more significant role in other operations. For instance, bulk techniques may be essential in relation to certain cyber security threats, or threats from foreign-based terrorist organizations. This has been acknowledged by the European Court of Human Rights. In Centrum for Rattvisa v Sweden, the Court accepted that the operation of a bulk interception regime 'in order to identify hitherto unknown threats to national security is one which continues to fall within States' margin of appreciation'.[128] Big Brother Watch, on the other hand, addressed externally focused threats and accepted, in principle, the appropriateness of bulk measures in this context.[129] In such circumstances it is for the state to demonstrate the necessity for such powers, and to detail why traditional alternatives are inadequate. In doing so, state agencies could develop a methodology for ascertaining the degree of indispensability of bulk powers in any given application. The existence, operation and credibility of this methodology could be a key focal point for oversight agencies.

Given the potential for harm, resource or efficiency savings cannot provide justification in and of themselves. It should be recalled that in situations where bulk powers cannot be justified, targeted surveillance measures may be initiated. As such, the benefits of, for example, communications data analysis are not necessarily denied to security agencies. The requirement is that such surveillance be initiated on the basis of reasonable suspicion.

Conclusion

This article has argued for the importance of defining the specific offences to which bulk communications data techniques may be applied. Such determinations should focus on activities that constitute a genuine threat to democratic institutions, for which extensive surveillance powers are warranted. This approach recognizes the utility of bulk communications data techniques, but avoids the pitfalls associated with attempting to determine the role played by such techniques in specific operations. While deliberations over acceptable thresholds for risk, and of resourcing for policing and security agencies, will no doubt continue, clarity in this regard will also provide guidance to the intelligence and security services, and help to protect against overreach. Importantly, this approach does not create an artificial distinction between intelligence and policing activities, but instead focuses on the actual crimes or activities being prevented. Other benefits include greater operational clarity than that which exists through the current under- standing of the strict necessity test, which focuses on utility in specific operations. A clear onus must be placed on the intelligence and security agencies to demonstrate the strict necessity requiring the use of such exceptional and far-reaching measures.

However, human rights concerns do not end with a clearer understanding of what 'serious crime' means in this context. Access to bulk communications data and oversight must be addressed. Both of these components are essential, not only with respect to preventing abuse, but also to ensuring public confidence. In particular, if access to bulk communications data is tightly circumscribed and accompanied by effective oversight, then the harm associated with surveillance and the chilling effect may be reduced. Active surveillance will be – and will be known to be – the exception and not the rule. Human rights case law establishes a number of relevant requirements in relation to both access and oversight.[130] These will not be discussed in detail here. Instead a few foundational elements may be highlighted.

The authority to conduct bulk communications data surveillance must be limited to those situations where it is 'strictly necessary in a democratic society', and should therefore be permissible only in relation to serious crime, as defined in the above discussion. It is equally essential that access to the product of any bulk communications data programme be correspondingly restricted. In most – if not all – situations, the request to initiate bulk surveillance must be linked to a defined operation, and access restricted to that same operation. This will ensure that information collected is ring-fenced, and is not re-purposed. This would not only mitigate a range of potential types of surveillance harm, but may also bring ancillary benefits with regard to conformity with good practice within data protection and data management regimes. Failure to restrict access appropriately undermines or negates the requirements imposed on the initial collection, potentially resulting in an extension of exceptional powers to non-exceptional incidents.

Oversight measures provide a key means of both preventing abuse and ensuring public confidence in the use of bulk powers. Accountability and the role of the courts are clearly important issues. However, it is equally essential that independent oversight bodies examine the day-to-day practice of those agencies involved in the use of bulk techniques,[131] and issue publicly available reports.[132] They should not only ensure that procedures are followed, but should also examine how information is stored, who has access to it, how data is processed, deleted, and so on. Future research into effective access and oversight regimes could build on these insights and thus add additional weight to the 'downstream' elements of bulk data handling that exist beyond the point of collection, yet exert additional potential for harm.

Chapter 5

Germany's Intelligence Reforms:
More Surveillance, Modest Restraints and Inefficient Controls

Thorsten Wetzling

Executive Summary

By December 2016, the most significant intelligence reform in recent German history was finally on the books.[1] It took more than a year of secret negotiations and a brief legislative process to codify important new rules about the practice, authorization and oversight of foreign data collection by the Bundesnachrichtendienst (BND), Germany's foreign intelligence agency. The reform sets new international standards in regard to the authorization procedures now required for the surveillance of non-national data and the legal requirements for Germany's participation in international intelligence cooperation. For the first time, there now exists a distinction between German nationals, EU nationals, and the rest of the world when it comes to restrictions on signals intelligence (SIGINT). At least de jure, Germany now requires the authorization of almost all strategic surveillance measures by a panel of jurists. By contrast, recent reforms in the United Kingdom or the U.S. offer no such standard for non-national data.

Despite this, the reform still marks a clear victory for the Chancellery and the German security and intelligence establishment. They drove the reform and pushed the de jure expansion of the BND's digital powers through the legislature despite numerous and widely reported scandals such as the careless disclosure of German and European strategic interests to the Five Eyes intelligence alliance and the warrantless spying on citizens, EU partners and international organizations. The reform placed much of the BND's foreign communications data surveillance on a legal footing but did not fix the country's woefully inadequate judicial oversight system. If anything, the reform paved the way for further retreat of judicial oversight in Germany. Its investment in more parliamentary oversight is helpful but not a sufficient response to the astonishing breadth of intelligence governance deficits left unaddressed. While the reform's provisions on the targeting of fellow Europeans and international intelligence cooperation are important steps in the right direction, they are also too weak to actually rein in the German spymasters.

I. Overview

This paper seeks to inform international readers about recent changes to German intelligence law. It depicts the political context of the reform followed by a brief summary of its main changes. Next, the paper elaborates on the reform's main achievements, its constitutionality and its substantial shortcomings. Thereafter, the focus turns to unresolved problems and open questions concerning the future practice of German foreign intelligence.

a) Codified and un-codified surveillance powers

The text introduces a number of key concepts used in German signals intelligence law and briefly accounts for the country's main legislative framework and its basic intelligence oversight architecture. The BND and the other 19 German intelligence services have a wide range of digital powers at their disposal.[2] Some powers are based in statute, while others are exercised by executive decree, i.e. without "the legal embodiment of the democratic will" (Born 2002: 17). Table 1 lists a few known powers that pertain to the interception of communications data.

Table 1: Some of the BND's surveillance powers and their legal basis

Surveillance of communications data of individual German citizens as well as residents and legal entities in Germany	Section 3 Art. 10 Law
Surveillance of communications data of foreign individuals on foreign territory	Not codified; secret executive decree
Strategic (untargeted) surveillance of communications data with either origin or destination in Germany	Section 5 Art. 10 Law
Strategic (untargeted) surveillance of communications data with neither origin nor destination in Germany	Art. 6 BND Law (2016 reform)
Computer Network Exploitation	Not codified; secret executive decree
Bulk Data Acquisition	Not codified; secret executive decree

The 2016 intelligence reform focused primarily on the practice of strategic surveillance (strategische Fernmeldeaufklärung). This term refers to the bundled collection of large quantities of communications data without concrete individual probable cause. It needs to be distinguished from surveillance measures that are directed at an individual suspect and his/her contacts. Furthermore, German SIGINT law distinguishes between different types of strategic surveillance measures. Whereas the strategic surveillance of international telecommunication data to and from Germany has long been codified and subjected to judicial review, the strategic surveillance of international communications data that has both its origin and destination outside of Germany (Ausland-Ausland-Fernmeldeaufklärung)–up until recently–lacked a comparable legal framework.[3] For easier reference and comparison, Table 2 summarizes Germany's legal and oversight framework for strategic surveillance that existed prior to the 2016 reform, while Table 3 depicts the newly established framework. The following sections will discuss this in greater detail. It's sufficient to say here that German intelligence legislation consists of a "complicated, scattered, and imperfect set of rules" (Gärditz 2017: 421).

b. Important distinctions in German intelligence law

An important norm to guide the practice and judicial oversight of surveillance by the intelligence services is Article 10 of the German Constitution (BasicLaw). It guarantees the privacy of correspondence, post and telecommunications as a fundamental "right that protects the rights holder against tapping, monitoring and recording of telecommunication contents [...] the analysis of their contents and the use of the data thus gained" (Deutscher Bundestag 2015: 2). Article 10 of the Basic Law primarily obligates the state to refrain from interfering with privacy. When telecommunication is being monitored, "a deep intrusion into the fundamental right to privacy takes place. The infringement is particularly severe given that the imperative secrecy of these measures means that the targeted individuals are excluded from the authorization procedure" (Ibid). Due to this, the German Constitution demands a clear legal basis for all such derogations. The Article 10 Law provides the required legal basis for this. Established in 1968, it defines the cases and scope for the three federal intelligence services to engage in different forms of communication surveillance and sets the legal framework for judicial oversight.

Another statute discussed in this paper is the BND Law.[4]. It provides the mandate for the BND and was substantially reformed in 2016 to include provisions on the practice, authorization and oversight of strategic foreign-foreign communications data surveillance as well as international SIGINT cooperation. As shown by Tables 2 and 3, the authorization and oversight process for strategic surveillance in German intelligence law differs significantly depending on whether the surveillance measure are deemed to affect German citizens or not. Prominent constitutional scholars argued in 2014 that the BND's strategic foreign-foreign communications data surveillance practice infringes upon the right to private communication guaranteed by Art 10 of the Basic Law. This right, they argued, protects not just German citizens but every person. According to their view, neither nationality of the communicating participants nor countries of residence are decisive criteria for the protection of civil rights (Bäcker 2014: 19). Rather, they argue, the key aspect is that German public authorities are bound by the provisions of the Basic Law at all times.

The German government and the 2016 reform did not adopt this position. Instead, the government argued that the right guaranteed by Article 10 of the Basic Law can be territorially restricted so as to protect only German citizens at home and abroad as well as residents and legal entities in Germany. This aspect as well as questions regarding the government's ability to distinguish clearly between national and non-national data and the effectiveness of its data minimization procedures will also be discussed later in the text.

c. Oversight institutions and the authorization process

Important German institutions of intelligence oversight are the Bundestag's permanent intelligence oversight committee (Parlamentarisches Kontrollgremium-PKGr) and the Trust Committee (Vertrauensgremium). The former performs mainly ex post review of intelligence policy whereas the latter's sole task is budget control. The G10 Commission-a quasi-judicial body of the Bundestag - performs judicial oversight on communications interception by the federal intelligence agencies. In addition, the German Federal Data Protection Authority (BfDI) performs reviews on the handling of data by the federal intelligence services. With the 2016 reform, the oversight landscape grew with the addition of the Independent Committee (Unabhängiges Gremium). It is tasked with performing reviews of the BND's strategic foreign-foreign communications data surveillance as to its legality and necessity. In addition, the reform created the institution of a permanent intelligence oversight commissioner (Ständiger Bevollmächtigter) and further intelligence oversight staff within the Bundestag's administration.

The typical authorization process for strategic surveillance begins with the BND requesting permission to intercept communications data from either the German Interior Ministry (BMI)[5] or the

Chancellery (Bundeskanzleramt, BKAmt).[6] The government then prepares surveillance orders and presents them to either the G10 Commission or the Independent Committee for judicial review, depending on the surveillance measure being sought. Following their legality and necessity assessment, the G10 Commission or the Independent Committee can then either accept these orders or call for their immediate termination.[7] Whether both commissions have sufficient mandates and resources to be effective in their review function will also be discussed in the sections below. What can be said from the outset is that neither the G10 Commission nor the Independent Committee is judicial bodies sui generis. Thus, unlike in the U.S. or in Sweden, "German intelligence law does not entail a preventive judicial control; this blunt desideratum remains a gaping wound in the institutional body of the German intelligence architecture." (Gärditz 2017: 431).

Table 2: Pre-reform framework for the BND's strategic surveillance

Practice	Foreign-Domestic Strategic Surveillance (Strategische Fernmeldeaufklärung)	Foreign-Foreign Strategic Surveillance (Ausland-Ausland-Fernmeldeaufklärung)
Law	Section 5 Art. 10 Law	Section 2.1 BND Law and secret interpretations
Surveillance Orders	BND requests them through the Interior Ministry	unregulated
Review Body & Composition	G10 Commission (4 honorary members, 4 deputies)	Only executive control (if at all)
Warrants	Default standard: Ex ante authorization with full knowledge of search terms	n/a

Oversight Mandate	Legality & necessity review; can prompt immediate end of measures deemed unlawful or unnecessary	n/a
Investigation Powers	Full access to premises & documents	n/a
Effective Remedy Procedure	Default standard: Ex post notifications	n/a
Data Minimization	DAFIS Filter System	DAFIS Filter System
Quantity Restriction	20 percent rule in Section 10.4 Art.10 Law	None

Table 3: Post-reform framework for the BND's strategic surveillance

Practice	Foreign-Domestic Strategic Surveillance (Strategische Fernmeldeaufklä- rung)	Foreign-Foreign Strategic Surveillance (Ausland-Ausland-Fernmelde-aufklärung)
Law	Art. 10 Law	BND Law
Surveillance Orders	BND requests them through Interior Ministry	BND requests them through Chancellery
Review Body & Composition	G10 Commission (4 honorary members, 4 deputies)	Independent Committee (UG) (3 members, 3 deputies)
Characterization	Judicial oversight by quasi-judicial body	Restricted judicial oversight by administrative body
Review Sessions	Once a month	Once every three months

Warrants	Default standard: Ex ante authorization with full knowledge of search terms	Default standard: Ex ante authorization with limited knowledge of search terms
Oversight Man- date	G10 Commission can prompt immediate end of measures deemed unlawful or unnecessary	UG can prompt immediate end of measures deemed unlawful or unnecessary
Investigation Powers	Full access to premises & documents	Not specified.
Effective Remedy Procedure	Default standard: Ex post notifications	No notifications.
Data Minimization	DAFIS Filter System	DAFIS Filter System
Quantity Restriction	20% rule in Section 10.4 Art. 10- Law	None

II. Context on the BND-reform

a. A compelling case for reform

The revelations by Edward Snowden resulting in the Bundestag's far-reaching intelligence inquiry provided the impetus for intelligence reform. The so-called NSA-inquiry brought to light major legal gaps, poor executive control and grave democratic deficits concerning the governance of signals intelligence in Germany. This has caused harm to German and European strategic interests and has led to unjustifiable spying on German and EU citizens, EU Member States and EU institutions as well as international organizations.

More specifically, it emerged in 2014 that Germany's foreign intelligence agency performed its single most important surveillance activity for decades without a clear legal framework, let alone independent authorization and oversight. The activity in question is the collection of communications data with its origin and destination outside of Germany (Ausland-Ausland-Fernmeldeaufklärung) – referred to in this paper as strategic foreign-foreign communications data surveillance.

It is estimated that this practice makes up to 90 percent of the BND's overall strategic surveillance activities (Löffelmann 2015: 1). Yet, despite being so important and despite regularly infringing upon the privacy rights of millions, German intelligence legislation lacked provisions concerning the authorization of collecting and handling of personal data. Instead, as shown in Table 2, prior to the 2016 reform, the BND intercepted, analyzed, stored and transferred most of its strategic surveillance data solely on the basis of a very broad provision in the BND Law and additional secret legal interpretations.[8] When questions regarding the legality of the BND's strategic foreign-foreign communications data surveillance became pressing in the NSA-inquiry, the government revealed a number of wide-ranging and underwhelming legal interpretations that it had used vis-à-vis the intelligence services and private companies.[9]

Prior to 2016, a significant part of Germany's SIGINT practices were also exempt from any form of independent oversight: No parliamentary oversight body, no judicial review commission and no data protection authority had any say on the BND's strategic foreign-foreign communications data surveillance. Instead, a very small circle within the executive single-handedly ordered the collection of data sets, with rights infringements numbering in the millions. The expenditure of public money notwithstanding, the BND's strategic surveillance practice had also never been independently evaluated for its effectiveness. Finally, the government has yet to show that it provides a sufficiently robust protection for data that is not meant to be subjected to strategic foreign-foreign communications surveillance.[10]

All these deficits emerged during the Bundestag's NSA-inquiry. As a result, the already tarnished public trust in the German security and intelligence establishment, the Bundestag's oversight mechanisms and the Chancellery's grip on executive control eroded even further.[11] To make things worse, Germany had also introduced a resolution at the United Nations for better privacy protection and intelligence oversight which, seen in conjecture with its own deficits in this realm, cast doubt on the credibility of Germany's foreign (cyber) policy at that time.

b. Driving factors

Facing sustained negative media coverage and increasing pressure for legal certainty from within the services and the telecommunication sector, the government needed a suitable response to growing calls for a radical overhaul of the country's intelligence legislation and governance structures. Yet, powerful voices not just within the intelligence community constantly warned that, if anything, the security threats Germany faces have grown in severity and complexity. To them, it was essential that the BND's powers remained untouched or better yet that the BND received significantly more technical and human resources to professionalize its electronic surveillance practice.[12]

In the end, the key players within the Chancellery realized that it was wishful thinking to believe that they could get away with no reform. The intelligence sector's actions –on a weekly basis – illustrated that this storm would simply not pass. The German public had also become much more aware of the Chancellery's central role in the governance of signals intelligence. Given that there was hardly any regulatory framework, let alone public scrutiny regarding its role in the formulation of the National Intelligence Priority Framework (Aufgabenprofil BND), the authorization of foreign intelligence collection and international intelligence cooperation, the Chancellery may have also found it increasingly difficult to refer to them in public without any reform.

In May 2014, three of the country's most renowned constitutional experts publicly rebuked the government's argument that the BND Law provided a sufficient legal basis for the BND's foreign intelligence collection practice. This aggravated existing concerns among members of the intelligence and security sector and national telecommunication providers. Upset by the legal limbo and out of genuine fear for litigation they pushed hard for a modern legal basis for the BND's surveillance powers. Different cases brought to the constitutional and administrative courts by ISP providers, the G10 Commission; the opposition parties within the inquiry committee as well as several NGOs may have also propelled the Chancellery to seek a reform prior to the next federal election and the conclusion of the parliamentary investigation in 2017.[13]

When the Chancellery publicly acknowledged "operational deficits" in the BND's foreign intelligence collection programs,[14] it became clear that an intelligence reform had to be prepared. The following minimal consensus quickly emerged among the ruling government coalition in the Bundestag: The BND's mandate needed an update; future data collection on European partners ought to be limited; and intelligence oversight was currently not fit for purpose.

However, actual recommendations on how to reverse engineer established signals intelligence machinery so as to better accommodate human rights, oversight and accountability standards were in very short supply. The press and the Bundestag were primarily concerned with the ongoing investigation of past malfeasances and the reporting on the BND's methods. This created a vacuum that the Chancellery took advantage of. It became the real driver behind intelligence reform, albeit operating from quite a different vantage point. From the fall of 2015 onward, a small circle of key players within the Chancellery, the BND, the German foreign, interior and justice ministries as well as a handful of members of parliament and their key advisors worked behind closed doors on the new rules for the BND and its overseers.

Unlike in the UK or in the Netherlands, the German government kept the matter very close to its chest and did not allow any form of pre-legislative scrutiny. The draft bill was presented to parliament on the day before its summer recess in July 2016. A public hearing followed where seven experts made a whole range of recommendations on how to improve the envisaged changes to the BND Law (Deutscher Bundestag 2016). Those recommendations had virtually no effect on the majority of the lawmakers. In October 2016, the Bundestag and the Bundesrat (the Federal

Council) adopted the bills without any significant changes. While the reform entered into force in December 2016, it will take time for the new institutions to become fully operational.[15]

c. Summary

The 2016 reform introduced a number of significant changes to existing German intelligence law. The summary below focuses on aspects deemed particularly relevant for international readers.[16]

1. New rules for strategic foreign-foreign communications data surveillance

The BND Law now includes several new provisions on the authorization, collection, handling, transfer and oversight of strategic foreign communications data surveillance. In so doing, Germany sets an important new international standard. Next to specifying the BND's mandate to intercept such data from within Germany (for transitioning traffic) it now also includes a provision on the use of such data that the BND obtained abroad (Section 7). The main takeaways from the new rules in Section 6-18 are:

Unrestricted metadata collection.

The BND's collection of metadata by means of strategic foreign-foreign communications data surveillance remains unrestricted. The retention of metadata is limited to six months. By contrast, content data may be retained for up to 10 years.[17]

Unrestricted acquisition and restricted collection of content data

As before, the BND will continue to acquire raw data without any de jure restrictions when intercepting foreign-foreign communications data in bulk. However, Section 6.2 now obligates the foreign service to use search terms when operationalizing ("collecting") content data from its data pool.[18] Yet, the law defines neither "search term" nor "telecommunication nets" any further. Obviously, this leaves significant operational latitude for the intelligence community. In addition, Section 12 (Eignungsprüfung) provides for an important exception to the general search term provision. "Telecommunication nets," according to this rule, may be temporarily tested in order to assess the quality of their output and to generate new search terms.

New content data protection hierarchy

In regard to the collection of content, the BND law distinguishes between four different groups for which different authorization procedures, data protection standards and oversight provisions apply. In terms of prioritization, these groups are:

- **Beneficiaries of G10 protection** (i.e. German nationals, domestic legal entities and persons on German territory):[19] The amended BND law stipulates that the collection of content and metadata from this group by means of strategic foreign-foreign communications data surveillance is not permissible (Section 6.4). Any electronic surveillance on this group is subject to the provisions of the Art 10 Law which entails stricter rules for the authorization, handling, judicial oversight as well as notification procedures.

- **Public institutions of the European Union and its Member States**: The use of selectors that target public bodies of EU member states or EU institutions is restricted to 12 warranted cases and requires orders that mention the individual search terms (Section 9.2).

- **EU citizens: The use of selectors that target EU citizens is restricted to 21 warranted cases**. Interception orders are not required to mention the individual search terms (Section 9.2).

- **Non-EU data**: The least restrictive regime governs the steering of search terms that aim at non-EU data. This is justifiable (a) to identify and respond to threats to Germany's domestic and external security; (b) maintains Germany's capacity to act and (c) other information relating to the government's secret national intelligence priority framework (Aufgabenprofil). The strategic foreign-foreign communication data surveillance must be administered on "telecommunication nets" the Chancellery identified in its interception orders. There is no requirement for search terms to be listed in such orders.

Table 4: Authorization criteria for targets of the BND's strategic surveillance

Group A	Group B	Group C	Group D
German citizens at home & abroad, all persons on German territory and domestic legal entities	Public institutions of EU-Bodies & Member States	EU citizens	Rest of the world
This group may not be subjected to strategic surveillance of foreign-foreign communications data. Any surveillance must be done in accordance with Art. 10 Law. (Except for incidental collection)	Group B may be targeted. This requires collection order that must identify search terms. Search terms may only be used if necessary for information related to 11 + 1 warranted cases:	Group C may be targeted. Requires collection order but no need to mention search terms therein. Search terms may only be used if necessary for information related to 20 + 1 warranted cases: eight circumstances under Section 5.1 Art.10-Law +	Group D may be targeted. Requires collection order but no need to mention search terms therein. Search terms can be used if necessary for information related to 3 + 1 very broad broad warranted cases three broad justifications

	eight circumstances under Section 5.1 Art.10-Law + three broad justifications (Section 6.1 BND Law) if needed for third country information of particular relevance to Germany's security. + data collection under Section 12 BND Law	three broad justifications (Section 6.1 BND Law) if needed for third country information of particular relevance to Germany's security. + nine justifications under Section 3.1 Art. 10-Law + data collection under Section 12 BND Law	(Section6.1 BND Law) withoutthe third country relevance caveat + data collection underSection 12
G10 judicial oversight & general notification requirement to allow effective remedy.	Ex ante authorization with knowledge of search terms & Chancellery notification requirement No notifications to surveillance targets.	Ex ante authorization without knowledge of search terms. No notifications to surveillance targets.	Ex ante authorization without knowledge of search terms No notifications to surveillance targets.

Table 5: Different justifications for strategic surveillance measures in German intelligence law

Three warranted cases of Section 6.1 BND Law
• Risks to the internal or external security of the Federal Republic of Germany; • Germany's ability to act; • Information on developments of foreign and security policy significance that relate to the National Intelligence Priority Framework
Eight warranted cases of Section 5.1 Art. 10 Law
• An armed attack against the nation • Intent to carry out acts of international terror • International proliferation of military weapons • Illegal import or sale of narcotics • Counterfeiting • International money laundering • Smuggling or trafficking of individuals • The international criminal, terrorist or state attack by means of malicious pro- grams on the confidentiality, integrity or availability of IT systems
Nine warranted cases of Section 3.1 Art. 10 Law
• Crimes of treason • Crimes that are a threat to the democratic state • Crimes that threaten external security • Crimes against national defense • Crimes against the security of NATO troops stationed in the Federal Republic of Germany • Crimes against the free democratic order as well as the existence or the security of the country. • Crimes under the Residence Act • Crimes under Sections 202a, 202b and 303a, 303b of the Criminal Code, in so far as they are directed against the internal or external security of the Federal • Republic of Germany, in particular against security sensitive bodies of vital institutions • Crimes under Section 13 of the Criminal Code

Ban on economic espionage. The BND Law introduced an explicit ban on the use of foreign-foreign communication surveillance for the purpose of economic espionage. It does not, however, define economic espionage or provide a list of practices that could be categorized as such.

2. A separate authorization and oversight regime.

The reform created the Independent Committee (Unabhängiges Gremium -UG), a second German authorization body for strategic surveillance. Situated at the Federal Court of Justice in Karlsruhe, the UG provides ex ante authorization of strategic foreign-foreign communications data surveillance by the BND. It consists of three members plus three deputies. Its president and one member must be judges at the Federal Court of Justice. The third member must be a federal public prosecutor at that court. The executive appoints the members of the Independent Committee (Section 16.2). It meets at least every three months and has the power to induce the immediate end to measures it finds unlawful or unnecessary.

3. Rules for international intelligence cooperation.

In regard to SIGINT cooperation between the BND and its foreign intelligence partners, the BND Law now contains a number of provisions that are also outstanding by international comparison. Sections 13-15 mark the first specific provisions on international intelligence cooperation in German intelligence law.

- Section 13.3 states that any new cooperation between the BND and foreign intelligence partners requires a prior written administrative agreement on the aims, then a true and the duration of the cooperation. This also includes an appropriations clause that the data may only be used for the purpose it was collected and that the use of the data must respect fundamental rule of law principles. Agreements also require a consultation among the foreign cooperation partners to comply with a data deletion request by the BND.

- Section 13.4 defines seven broad permissible aims for new international SIGINT cooperation involving the BND. These include 'information on political, economic or military developments abroad that are relevant for foreign and security' to 'comparable cases'. SIGINT cooperation agreements with EU, EFTA and NATO partners require the approval of the Chancellery. Agreements with other countries require approval by the head of the Chancellery. The executive is required to inform the parliamentary intelligence oversight body about all such agreements.

- Sections 26-30 introduce new provisions on SIGINT databases. The BND can run joint databases (Section 27) or contribute to foreign-run databases (Section 30). The BND's cooperation with foreign partners on databases is only permissible when (a) deemed particularly relevant for Germany's foreign and security interests; (b) basic rule of law principles are being upheld within partnering states (c) if all partners agree to honor the reciprocity principle (Section 26.2). The Chancellery's authorization and parliamentary oversight notification obligations are the same as those for the SIGINT cooperation agreements. There is a similar requirement that the aims and forms of cooperation on joint databases are documented in writing form to the operation.

- Section 28 further requires that the BND must keep detailed separate file arrangement documentation for each database it uses with foreign intelligence partners and for which it is in charge. The German Federal Data Protection Authority (BfDI) must be consulted prior to the installation of a new database file arrangement. It may review the creation of new databases by the BND as well as the data that the BND contributes to joint databases.

4. New rules and institutions for parliamentary intelligence oversight.

The reform also introduces significant changes to the law on and future practice of parliamentary intelligence oversight (PKGr Law). Most notably:

- It created the new institution of a permanent intelligence oversight coordinator. As the nine members of the parliamentary intelligence oversight committee often lack the time, resources and knowledge to perform their important mandate, the coordinator can now perform investigations on their behalf. He or she can also be tasked for additional budget control by the Bundestag's Trust Committee. The coordinator prepares the public reports by the intelligence oversight body and takes part in the monthly G10-sessions, the meetings of the parliamentary oversight body and the Trust Committee.

- It further clarified the reporting obligations of the executive. It has to report on the general activities of the three federal intelligence services but also on developments of particular relevance. The amended law now provides three examples for the latter: (a) notable changes to Germany's foreign and domestic security situation; (b) internal administrative developments with substantial ramifications for the pursuit of the services' mandate and (c) singular events that are subject to political discussions or public reporting (Section 4.1 PKGr Law).

- The reform will also create more than a dozen full-time positions for intelligence oversight within the Bundestag's administration. As of yet, these positions have not been filled and there is little information on what is planned for them in the future.

III. Analysis

The following section provides a critical analysis of Germany's recent intelligence reform. The discussion begins with what the author sees as true improvements in the reform. Especially, when compared to recent surveillance reforms in other countries, Germany's expansion of the authorization procedure to non-national data and its new requirements for SIGINT cooperation stand out as progressive.

a. The improvements in intelligence reform

Democratic legitimacy for a key SIGINT practice

The reform now provides a specific legal footing for a significant part of the BND's SIGINT activities. Given the magnitude of past deficits and the ubiquitous calls for a better legal framework, this may not seem like a major achievement. Yet despite the reform's many shortcomings, it is a fact that many European countries, let alone nations throughout the world, operate according to intelligence laws that do not contain detailed provisions on the practice of strategic communications data surveillance, let alone restrictions and democratic oversight on the collection of foreigners' data by national intelligence services.[21] At the very least, by means of this reform, the German parliament has now democratically legitimized almost the entire practice of the BND's strategic communications data surveillance.

Measures' legality and necessity can be challenged

Furthermore, the reform provides ex ante authorization and some ex post control provisions. Thus, de jure, the reform offers the possibility to challenge these measures on grounds of legality or necessity by jurists that are not bound by instructions from the executive.

Rules on international intelligence cooperation

By international comparison, the reform includes detailed provisions governing the BND's future SIGINT cooperation with foreign intelligence partners. The BND leadership must seek written agreements from foreign partners covering a number of aspects that, by and large, aim to restrict the BND's participation in measures that would be deemed unlawful if performed solely under German jurisdiction. Moreover, next to attaching a number of broad conditions to future SIGINT cooperation agreements, the reform also introduces specific rules on joint databases, particularly those run by the BND. For the latter, the German Federal Data Protection Authority's review mandate covers all the data that the BND contributes to joint databases with foreign partners.

New ministerial responsibilities

The reformed BND Law now requires more documentation for individual decisions and includes a number of accountability provisions for the Chancellery's or–as the case may require the Head of the Chancellery's steering of SIGINT measures. For example, future interception orders must refer to telecommunication nets determined by the Chancellery. The use of selectors targeting EU institutions or EU Member States requires prior notification of the Chancellery and new SIGINT agreements as well as the maintenance of joint databases must be approved by the Chancellery. These and other provisions further reduce the risk of plausible deniability by the executive vis-à-vis its foreign service.

b. The reform's contested privacy discrimination

The reform of the BND Law is based on the premise that the right to private communication as guaranteed in the German constitution (Art. 10 of the Basic Law) can be territorially restricted so as to protect only German citizens at home and abroad, residents and domestic legal entities in Germany. In other words, the reform presumes that the privacy infringements for non- Germans caused by these surveillance measures can be administered with significantly less safeguards compared to those afforded to Germans (See Table 4 above).

The constitutionality of this restricted interpretation of Art. 10 Basic Law is highly contested and has yet to be answered by the Constitutional Court. Clearly, the drafters of the intelligence reform took a significant risk: In case their interpretation of the limited territorial reaches of Art. 10 of the Basic Law fail to convince the Constitutional Court, they will have to revise almost the entire 2016 reform. This is because the reform and its explanatory memorandum carefully avoid any specific reference to Art. 10 of the Basic Law as well as to the existing regime for the authorization and judicial oversight of strategic surveillance (Art. 10 Law).

Instead of adding new rules for strategic foreign-foreign communications data surveillance into the existing Art. 10 Law and instead of strengthening the G10 Commission's mandate, the government created a whole new parallel legal and oversight framework with the amendments to the BND Law. The ensuing discrimination against privacy protections and the fragmentation of the German oversight landscape could have been avoided. It would have been possible to extend the basic right to private communication under Art. 10 of the German Constitution to foreigners abroad without necessarily extending the ex post notification practice to them. But this would have come at the cost of extending the territorial reach of Art. 10 and this was an option the government tried to avoid at all costs.

Whereas the German Constitutional Court has not equivocally positioned itself on the territorial reach of Art. 10 Basic Law question in the past, it will soon have to take a stance. Litigation is currently being prepared by the Society for Civil Rights (Gesellschaft für Freiheitsrechte, GFF) that will require a definite position by the court.

c. Some of the reform's many deficiencies

Insufficient Judicial Oversight

The reform created a second authorization body for strategic communications data surveillance by the BND. Despite being staffed by professional jurists and its proximity to the Federal Court of Justice in Karlsruhe, the Independent Committee (UG) is neither independent nor a court. Not only are its three members and deputies appointed by the executive, one of the three members will also be a public prosecutor from the Federal Public Prosecutor's Office. This is problematic for potential conflicts of interest. Instead, it may be referred to as an administrative body tasked with the ex ante authorization of the newly codified surveillance measures.

While the BND-reform created the UG, the new provisions say very little on its actual oversight powers. By comparison, the G10 commission is not only tasked to authorize surveillance measures but it also has the authority to review the collection, subsequent data handling and use of all personal data related to the surveillance measures. In order to do so, the G10 Commission has guaranteed access to all documents, saved data and data management programs used in conjunction with surveillance measures as well as access to any premises used for SIGINT purposes by all three federal intelligence agencies (Section 15.5 Art. 10 Law). By contrast, the BND Law makes no mention of such judicial oversight powers for the UG. Clearly, the UG is not meant to engage in any in-depth judicial oversight. Interestingly, however, the law does grant the UG the authority to conduct random checks whether the search terms used by the BND for the targeting of EU-data corresponds to the restrictions articulated in Section 6.3.

Apart from the missing provisions on the UG's actual oversight powers, one can also express serious concerns regarding the authorization procedure. More specifically, when the UG assesses the legality and necessity of a surveillance measure it may do so on the basis of interception orders that do not list the search terms. Any legality and necessity assessment it makes without knowledge of the search terms is likely to lack credibility and substance.

Further fragmentation of German intelligence oversight system

Instead of streamlining the existing oversight landscape, the reform has fragmented it further. Next to the Trust Committee (budget oversight), the permanent parliamentary oversight body, the G10 Commission and the Federal Data Protection Authority, democratic intelligence oversight will now also be administered by two new institutions: the Independent Committee and the Parliamentary Oversight Commissioner. As indicated, the fact that Germany now hosts two separate authorization bodies for strategic surveillance– one in Berlin (G10 Commission) and one in Karlsruhe (UG) – can only be explained when seen as a corollary to the government's position on the restricted territorial reach of Art. 10 of the Basic Law. It would have made much more sense to just extend the mandate of the existing G10 Commission. However, not only did the G10 Commission show its own deficits (see next section), it had also displayed a newly-acquired audacity to publicly challenge the government.[22]

While the reform has introduced limited measures to facilitate the exchange of information among oversight bodies – for example, the oversight commissioner's right to attend the different meetings of the Trust Committee, the parliamentary oversight body and the G10 Commission – many members still refer to their respective institutions as silos. Individual members of the G10 Commission are not regularly in touch with the members of the parliamentary oversight body and the reform has not foreseen any specific exchange between the Independent Committee and the G10 Commission. Given the similarity of interception orders and the similar role of telecommunication providers compelled to assist the government, it would certainly be useful for both bodies to be more systematically aligned, possibly even conducting joint assessments and visits on the premises of the foreign service.

Soft restrictions

As previously shown, the new provisions in the BND Law use unduly broad definitions when regulating aspects that are meant to restrict surveillance. For example, consider the minimal requirements for search terms used to collect information on non-EU data (Section 6.1) or the list of permissible goals for new international SIGINT cooperation agreements (Section 13.4). What, one may ask, falls under information required to secure the Federal Republic's capacity to act (Section 6.1) or what defines 'comparable cases' that may give rise to new international SIGINT cooperation (Section 13.4)? Also, the rules on future international SIGINT cooperation agreement need only be unilaterally declared once at the beginning. Follow-up procedures to monitor the adherence to those rules have not been foreseen.

Equally concerning is the fact that the law provides no restrictions on the extensiveness regarding the acquisition of data from "telecommunication nets" (Section 6.1). Hence, Germany's Foreign Service may acquire as much raw data as it likes or its resources allow. Compare this, for example, with Section 10.4 Art. 10-Law which stipulates that interception orders for strategic communication that may also target national data must identify the geographical area for which information is being sought and also the communication channels (transmission paths). Furthermore, for any strategic surveillance on foreign-domestic communication there is the requirement that the data subjected to surveillance must not exceed 20 percent of the overall capacity of the communication channels identified in the order (Section 5 Art-10-Law).[23]

The BND Law also does not clarify what may be defined as "search term" and how these terms may be used in practice. It may be understandable that an intelligence law does not provide detailed information on operational procedures which can also rapidly change over time, the mere reference to "search term" does provide ample latitude for the intelligence sector to use the most powerful regular expressions, especially if oversight and review bodies lack the knowledge and resources to review the use of regular expressions in surveillance programs.

Abstract notification requirements instead of more transparency

Consider briefly the U.S. government's Implementation Plan for the Principles for Intelligence Transparency and its various accompanying measures that seek to make "information publicly available in a manner that enhances public understanding of intelligence activities".[24] For example, a Tumblr site (IC on the Record) features among other declassified documents dozens of orders and opinions by the U.S. Foreign Intelligence Surveillance Court (FISC)–the rough equivalent of Germany's quasi-judicial G10-Commission. In Germany, the G10 Commission itself has no reporting obligations. Instead, the parliamentary intelligence oversight body reports annually to the German Parliament on the measures performed in conjunction with the Art 10 Law. Those reports are public but they only provide rudimentary factual information about G10 authorizations rather than the Commission's underlying decisions and interpretations of the law. For example, the 2015 G10 report states that in regard to the steering of search terms per threat category per six months, the G10 Commission authorized 949 search terms that fall into the category of "international terrorism."[25]

In regard to the foreign surveillance measures codified in the amended BND Law, Section 16.6 only requires that the Independent Committee informs the parliamentary oversight body about its work at least every six months. There are no further requirements in the law about the content and format, let alone public documentation of such reporting.

d. *The reform's important omissions*

No overhaul for the opaque German intelligence legislation

German intelligence law remains a mess. It consists of numerous individual pieces of legislation that are rarely straightforward and a challenge even to experienced lawyers. The recent intelligence reform offered a chance to design a comprehensive, modern intelligence law from scratch but that was never seriously considered. The second-best option would have been to insert the new provisions on strategic foreign-foreign communications data surveillance into the existing law on the authorization and judicial oversight of strategic surveillance. For the reasons outline above, this was politically inopportune and therefore carefully avoided. The fact that the actual reform further fragmented the oversight landscape and has rendered the body of German intelligence legislation even less comprehensible has caused little concern.

No reform of the G10 Commission

Worse still, this also meant that the numerous legal and institutional deficits that exist with the system for the authorization and judicial oversight of strategic surveillance as regulated for in the Art. 10 Law were left unaddressed by the reform. For example, the G10 Commission (a) still lacks sufficient resources and does not review the handling of data by the intelligence services, (b) remains staffed by four honorary fellows who come together only once a month to authorize a stack of inception orders; (c) still operates without adversarial proceedings (i.e. there is no-one within the commission to present the views of those subjected to surveillance and argue for less infringing measures) and; (d) the abuse-prone and anachronistic rule that restricts the collection of foreign-domestic surveillance data to a maximum of 20 percent of the capacity of the pertinent communication channels also remained in place.[26]

Other bulk powers not legislated for

Despite all the valid criticism that the British intelligence reform received, Westminster did legislate for other bulk powers. By contrast, the BND Law says nothing about the Foreign Service's hacking powers (Computer Network Exploitation). The BND's acquisition of existing databases from the commercial sector also remains unlegislated. Furthermore, German intelligence law continues to leave the so-called 'reine Auslandsaufklärung', i.e. the BND's strategic surveillance against foreigners on foreign soil without any search term requirements, unregulated (Graulich 2017: 47).

Effectiveness of strategic surveillance still not assessed

Do these privacy infringements numbering in the millions actually pay off and offer a concrete security gain? Unfortunately, despite such calls by the Chancellor's coalition partner,[27] the reform did not establish an independent evaluation procedure so as to assess the effectiveness of strategic surveillance and the accuracy of the data minimization programs. Thus, the following two important claims cannot be verified :(1) This huge surveillance infrastructure that was built and operationalized in the shadows of democratic oversight produces actionable intelligence and; (2) our agents only get to see lawfully collected data. The current oversight institutions lack the mandate and the IT-resources to perform any such evaluation. Parliamentarians lack the imagination and the political will to use their legislative and budgetary powers to close this pressing gap. Next to the American example where the Presidential Civil Liberties Oversight Board (PCLOB) performed effectiveness investigations, consider also the Dutch independent oversight board CTIVD. It has recently announced a new project to review "the possibilities of systemic oversight on the acquisition, analysis and deletion of large amounts of data."[28]

No limit to metadata collection

A draft version of the BND bill was at one point circulated which included restrictions on the collection, use and transfer of metadata within the framework of strategic foreign-foreign communications data collection. Yet, these restrictions were removed from the bill presented to parliament. Given the importance of metadata for modern surveillance and warfare, and given that metadata by itself is enough to construct highly accurate personal profiles; it is regrettable that the reform did not introduce any limits on the BND here.

e. Open questions

Sufficient technical prowess to curb incidental collection?

The reform assumes the BND's technical prowess great enough to neatly distinguish between different data groups for which different authorization and oversight regimes apply. Yet the tools used for modern communication and its transmission defy coarse categorization. This brings up the question of data minimization. The BND uses the same automated filter program (DAFIS) to sift through the acquired raw data. Even if – and without the effectiveness review mentioned above this is pure guesswork – the filter does reach an accuracy level of 98.5 percent this would still mean that the BND incidentally collects, uses and transfers thousands of datasets daily without respecting the law that requires G10 protections and notifications.[29]

Interestingly, Section 10.4 already alludes to incidental collection of content and metadata and requires the immediate deletion of wrongfully obtained data or the notification of the G10 Commission in case the data will be retained. Here the drafters used a somewhat twisted logic: In the pursuit of strategic foreign-foreign communications data collection, the BND must not collect data from German citizens at home or abroad, residents or legal German entities (Section 6.4). If it does (Section 10.4) it must delete that data or inform the G10 Commission if it retains that data. With filters working to 100 percent, there would be no need for this. Given that it will continue to happen, it adds – at least de jure – significantly to the workload of the understaffed G10 Commission. The following table summarizes the wide range of shortcomings with the recent German intelligence reform discussed in the previous section.

Table 6: Selection of post foreign intelligence reform deficits in Germany

Insufficient judicial oversight powers and resources	Further fragmenta-tion of the intelligence oversight architec-ture	Weak restrictions on surveil-lance	Lack of transpar-ency and abstract reporting require-ments	No adver-sarial pro-ceedings at either G10 Commis-sion or the UG
Severe defi-cits with the implemen-tation of Art. 10 Law remain un-addressed	Many other sur-veillance powers remain un-legislated	No inde-pendent evaluation of the ef-fectiveness of foreign surveil-lance tools	Unlimited metadata collection for mea-sures under the BND Law	Sig-nificant amount of incidental Collec-tion due to filter inaccura-cies

IV. Conclusion

Democracies need strong and agile security services to guard against a number of increasingly networked threats. International cooperation among national intelligence services is fundamentally important for our security. Yet, given the invasiveness of modern surveillance, intelligence services ought to be subjected to effective democratic oversight. This promotes rights-based and legitimate intelligence governance that is vital to the social fabric of any democracy. By and large, Germany's recent intelligence reform did not pave the way toward meeting this important objective. It was designed, first and foremost, to provide legal certainty for intelligence service members and private companies involved in pursuit of strategic surveillance.

Legal clarity and the rule of law were not the key objectives of this reform. In fact, the reform created a number of new problems and left major deficits unresolved. Judicial oversight of intelligence, which in theory is the most useful tool to rein in rogue elements given its concrete and immediate sanctioning power, have been hollowed out with this reform. Just take the new Independent Committee as an example. With its creation and the missed opportunity to address the grave deficits of the G10 Commission, the reform unduly fragmented the German oversight landscape and contributed to the retreat of judicial intelligence control. A more fragmented, albeit more resourceful, system of parliamentary intelligence oversight is hardly the appropriate response to Germany's problems with intelligence governance. The reform also did not address the urgent need to provide for an independent evaluation of the effectiveness of the many surveillance programs either. Besides, many key questions surrounding the use of data gained from strategic surveillance remain within the sole and unchecked responsibility of the executive. Despite being in effect since December 2016, the reform is also far from being fully implemented at the time of writing.[30]

However, especially with a view to recent intelligence reform in other countries, Germany's reform has also set a few benchmarks that deserve further recognition. Its intelligence laws now cover a far greater spectrum of SIGINT activities than ever before. The required authorization of foreign-foreign surveillance programs by a panel of jurists also sets a new international standard. By comparison, the U.S. FISA Court only reviews surveillance programs that impact US-nationals.[31] While the terms used to restrict surveillance on non-nationals are vague and the actual investigation powers of the Independent Committee unclear, the BND Law – unlike other European intelligence laws–does give special protection to EU citizens. Also in regard to the new requirements for international intelligence cooperation, Germany has gone further with its reform than many other democracies. The reform brought new documentation and authorization requirements for the executive which may lead to more political accountability, a core problem identified by all intelligence inquiries in Germany over the past decade.

German Intelligence Reform, June 2017, Policy Brief. Thorsten Wetzling. This paper is subject to a Creative Commons license (CC BY-SA). The redistribution, publication, transformation or translation of publications of the Stiftung Neue Verantwortung which are marked with the license "CC BY-SA". Thorsten Wetzling directs the Privacy Project at the Stiftung Neue Verantwortung. Thorsten holds a doctorate degree in political science from the Graduate Institute of International and Development Studies in Geneva. The Stiftung Neue Verantwortung (SNV) is an independent think tank that develops concrete ideas as to how German politics can shape technological change in society, the economy and the state.

Chapter 6

Theorizing Surveillance in the UK Crime Control Field

Michael McCahill

Abstract

Drawing upon the work of Pierre Bourdieu and Loic Wacquant, this paper argues that the demise of the Keynesian Welfare State (KWS) and the rise of neo-liberal economic policies in the UK has placed new surveillance technologies at the centre of a reconfigured "crime control field" (Garland, 2001) designed to control the problem populations created by neo-liberal economic policies (Wacquant, 2009 a). The paper also suggests that field theory could be usefully deployed in future research to explore how wider global trends or social forces, such as neo-liberalism or bio-power, are refracted through the crime control field in different national jurisdictions. We conclude by showing how this approach provides a bridge between society-wide analysis and micro-sociology by exploring how the operation of new surveillance technologies is mediated by the "habitus" of surveillance agents working in the crime control field and contested by surveillance subjects.

Keywords: Capital; crime control; resistance; surveillance

1. Introduction

Surveillance, defined as the "collection and analysis of information about populations in order to govern their activities" (Haggerty & Ericson, 2006, p. 3), has always been a central feature of policing and criminal justice. This includes the "direct supervision" of subject populations in prisons and probation work and the accumulation of "coded information"(Giddens, 1985) which began in the nineteenth century when fingerprints, photographs and files were collated by criminal justice practitioners. Over the last two decades however the advent of computer databases, surveillance cameras and other technological advances are said to have given rise to a "new surveillance"[1] (Marx, 2002) comprising of "surveillant assemblages" (Haggerty & Ericson, 2000) which operate well beyond the confines of the central state. In an attempt to make sense of these developments, the theoretical literature has been dominated by Foucaultian and Deleuzian-inspired perspectives on "discipline" (Foucault, 1977) and "control" (Deleuze, 1992).

As Lyon (1993, p. 655) points out, for many writers "the idea of exploiting uncertainty in the observed as a way of ensuring their subordination has obvious resonance with current electronic technologies that permit highly unobtrusive monitoring of data subjects in a variety of social contexts". For other writers, the disciplinary model of surveillance eventually proved too inflexible "to organize the mobile labour forces and financial flows of complex information economies" (Bogard, 2012, p. 33). Thus, while for some writers the emergence of new surveillance technologies is consistent with the "disciplinary power" and "self-governing capabilities" identified by Foucault (Staples & Decker, 2008), for others disciplinary power has been replaced with "modulation" which works through models, simulation, codes, statistical tracking, and new methods of social sorting (Bogard, 2012, pp. 32-33).

The central argument presented here is that the Focuaultian and Deleuzian-inspired literature outlined above does not adequately address the politics of surveillance by explaining why or how new surveillance technologies have come to play such a central role in contemporary society and in particular how they have become central to policing and criminal justice. As Haggerty (2006, p. 34) points out, in the Foucaultian literature, "the movement of panoptic principles into new settings" is "often presented as entirely friction-less" and lacking any "sense of a surveillance politics".

Similarly, Deleuzian-inspired accounts of the emergence of networked and flexible forms of control in response to the global system of capital (Bogard, 2006) operate at a very high level of abstraction and consequently fail to explore how wider global trends or social forces, such as neo-liberalism or bio-power, are refracted through the crime control field in different national jurisdictions. To address these questions, we situate the emergence of new surveillance technologies within "fields of struggle", defined by Bourdieu "as a structured space of positions in which the positions and their interrelations are determined by the distribution of different kinds of resources or "capital" (Thompson, 1991, p. 14). We begin at the macro level by showing how globalizing forces and wider social changes are filtered through the "field of power"[2] in different national jurisdictions.

Next, we argue that the demise of the Keynesian Welfare State (KWS) and the rise of neo-liberal economic policies in the UK has placed new surveillance technologies at the centre of a reconfigured "crime control field" (Garland, 2001) de-signed to control the problem populations created by neo-liberal economic policies (Wacquant, 2009a). Finally, we show how field theory provides a bridge between society-wide analysis and micro-sociology by showing how the operation of new surveillance technologies is mediated by the "habitus"[3] of surveillance agents and surveillance subjects. But first we explain how and why we intend to use this approach to make sense of contemporary developments.

2. Why "Field" Theory?

In an early paper entitled, "The Genesis of the Bureaucratic Field", Pierre Bourdieu (1984) extends Max Weber's definition of the state as an institution "which possesses a monopoly over the legitimate use of (physical) violence", by adding that the bureaucratic field "also monopolizes the use of 'symbolic violence'" (Ben-son, 2005, p. 93). For Bourdieu, symbolic violence is the power to "constitute the given" (Bourdieu, 1991, p. 170) and refers to the state's "ability to make appear as natural, inevitable, and thus apolitical, that which is a product of historical struggle and human invention" (Loveman, 2005, p. 1655). From this perspective, the development of bureaucratic administration and the use of "civil registration and related forms of state identification of individuals are at the core of modern states' capacity to exercise symbolic power" (Loveman, 2005, p. 1679).

In this respect, Bourdieu's early paper on the state complements the work of other social theorists who have documented how surveillance originally emerged in the context of state bureaucracy, policing and government administration (Dandeker, 1990; Lyon, 1994). However, while Bourdieu used field theory to explore a wide-range of semi-autonomous and increasingly specialized spheres of action, such as the fields of politics, religion, and cultural production, he did not write about the "crime control field" (Garland, 2001) which makes up a key component of the "right hand of the state" (Wacquant, 2009a, p. 289; see also Page, 2013), nor did he have anything to say about the emergence of a "surveillance society" which has seen surveillance proliferate well beyond the bureaucratic field to become a routine and mundane feature that is "embedded in every aspect of life" (Lyon, 2001, p. 1).

In recent years however a number of writers have used field theory to analyze penal transformation in the age of neo-liberalism. Didier Bigo (2000, 2002), for example, has outlined the emergence of a transnational field of security professionals across the European Union involved in the "management of unease" (Bigo, 2002, p. 64). This approach has also been used by Dupont (2004, p. 85) who draws upon Bourdieu's notion of "capitals" (economic, social, cultural and symbolic) to explore how these resources can be "used as strategic assets to acquire or maintain a dominant position with-in security networks".

Garland (2001) meanwhile combines "field" theory with "governmentality" (Foucault, 1991) to argue that recent transformations in policing, punishment, sentencing and crime prevention "can best be grasped by viewing them as interactive elements in a structured field of crime control and criminal justice" (Garland, 2001, p. x). Finally, Wacquant (2009) has drawn upon Bourdieu's distinction between the "left hand" of the state (e.g. education, health, social assistance) and the "right hand" of the state (e.g. police, justice, and correctional administrations) (Bourdieu, 1998, p. 2) to examine the fusion of penal policy and welfare policy to manage the problem populations generated by neo-liberal economic policies.

One of the recurring criticisms levelled at Bourdieu's writings on the "bureaucratic field" is that he tends to generalise from the case of the (strong and centralised) French state and consequently "fails to speak to those in the Anglophone world who have experienced over thirty years of the rolling back of the state by neo-liberal governments" (A. Scott, 2013, p. 65). From this perspective, notions of "nodal governance" (Johnston & Shearing, 2003) or "governmentality" (Foucault, 1991) are much more suitable for theorizing the emergence of "surveillant assemblages" (Haggerty & Ericson, 2000) which operate beyond the confines of the bureaucratic field. However, following A. Scott (2013), we argue that it possible to use Bourdieu's parochialism (regarding his generalisation from the "strong" French state) to counter our own (Anglo-phone) parochialism regarding the "weak" neo-liberal state (A. Scott, 2013). In this respect, Bourdieu's writings on the bureaucratic field provide a means of critically engaging with the Foucualtian and Deleuzian literature which underestimates how neo-liberal strategies of privatization can serve to strengthen the position of political elites (A. Scott, 2013).

From this perspective, law and order campaigns and the introduction of new laws and surveillance measures "reassert the authority of the state and shore up the deficit of legitimacy officials suffer when they abandon the mission of social and economic protection established during the Fordist-Keynesian era" (Wacquant, 2010, p. 198). At the same time, this approach avoids economic reductionism or conspiracy theory[4], focusing instead on how social fields emerge as the result of on-going struggles between actors whose aim is to set "the rules that govern the different social games (fields) and, in particular, the rules of reproduction of these games" (Wacquant, 1993, p. 42). The use of field theory outlined above we argue provides a useful theoretical framework for examining the politics of surveillance in the UK crime control field. However, there are two caveats to our use of this approach to theorize current surveillance practice. Firstly, while much of the criminological literature has focused on state surveillance and policing, this is too restrictive for an analysis of the new surveillance which increasingly operates across state and non-state institutions.

To avoid this limitation we use Garland's (2001) broader definition of the "crime control field". This includes "the formal controls exercised by the state's criminal justice agencies and the informal social controls that are embedded in everyday activities and interactions in civil society" (2001, p. 5). This more expansive conception of the crime control field allows us to examine the social impact of new surveillance in both the penal sec-tor of the bureaucratic field (e.g. prisons, probation and policing) and in the wider society which has seen new surveillance measures introduced in schools, universities, shopping malls, airports etc. (Simon, 2007).

Secondly, the question of how those on the receiving end of surveillance experience and respond to being monitored has received relatively little attention (although see Marx, 2003). For instance, in his account of how penal sanction and welfare supervision have merged "into a single apparatus for the cultural capture and behavioural control of marginal populations", Wacquant (2009 a, p. xix) explains how his approach "does not survey efforts to resist, divest, or divert the imprint of the penal state from below". To address this issue we draw upon recent ethnographic research de-signed to explore how a diverse range of groups experience and respond to being monitored by the new surveillance technologies that are currently used in the crime control field (McCahill & Finn, 2014).

We situate the emergence of surveillance within "fields of struggle", arguing that the distribution of various forms of "capital"—economic, social, cultural and symbolic—operate as a range of goods or resources that structure the dynamics of surveillance practices and power relations in the crime control field. By doing this we also extend Bourdieu's conceptual toolkit by introducing the term surveillance capital to illustrate how surveillance subjects utilize everyday forms of cultural know-how acquired through first-hand experience of power relations to challenge the very same power relations. However, before we examine the micro-politics of resistance, we need to situate the emergence of new surveillance in a wider political context.

3. The Global Diffusion of Surveillance—the Case of CCTV Surveillance Cameras

As Murakami Wood (2009, p. 181) has argued, generalized descriptions of a surveillance society often under-play the "immense cultural and geographic variety of surveillance societies" (emphasis added). Bourdieu's work is useful here because he "explodes the vacuous notion of 'society' and replaces it with those of field and social space". For Bourdieu, "fields of struggle" are relatively autonomous social spaces "that cannot be collapsed under an overall societal logic" (Bourdieu & Wacquant, 1992, p. 17) such as "modernity" or "post-modernity", or, we might add, the "surveillance society". Globalizing forces and wider social change, for ex-ample, are always filtered through the political and juridical fields of different national jurisdictions. Comparative work conducted by criminologists on the uneven global diffusion of the "new punitiveness[5] may be useful here for exploring the diffusion of new surveillance.

For instance, in their comparative study of criminal justice in twelve different countries, Cavadino and Dignan (2006) constructed a typology of political economy which showed major differences between neo-liberal (USA, South Africa, England and Wales, Australia, New Zealand), conservative-corporatist (Germany, France, Italy, and the Netherlands), social democratic (Sweden and Finland), and oriental-corporatist countries (Japan). In short, they found that neo-liberal countries were more punitive (exhibiting higher prison rates, lower age of criminal responsibility, and adoption of privatization policies), followed by conservative corporatist, social democratic and oriental corporatist (in Lacey, 2008, pp. 44-45). These findings have been supported by Lacey (2008) in her "comparative institutional analysis" which showed that Liberal Market Economies (LMEs) (especially the UK and USA) adopted more exclusionary criminal justice systems than Coordinated Market Economies (CMEs) (north-western Europe, Scandinavia and Japan).

Any attempt to address similar questions in relation to the global diffusion of new surveillance would re-quire systematic comparative research. However, there are one or two studies that allow us to raise some tentative questions or hypotheses that may guide future research. For instance, while research conducted on the rise of CCTV surveillance in Europe by the Urbaneye project found a general diffusion of surveillance cameras throughout European society, the growth of these systems in countries such as Germany and Norway was restricted due to the contrasting legal and constitutional environments of the juridical fields (see Norris, McCahill, & Murakami Wood, 2004, p. 121).

Thus, while the legal context in the UK is extremely permissive, privacy rights in CMEs such as Denmark and Norway are constitutionally enshrined. The latter also have strong data protection regimes to regulate the introduction and use of new surveillance measures such as CCTV surveillance cameras (see Norris et al., 2004, p. 121). The uneven proliferation of "new surveillance" must also be situated in a wider socio-economic context. Thus, whereas CMEs are "premised on incorporation" and "the need to reintegrate of-fenders onto society and economy", LMEs are based on flexibility and innovation which means that "under conditions of surplus unskilled labor…the costs of a harsh, exclusionary criminal justice system are less than they would be in a coordinated market economy" (Lacey, 2008, p. 59).

It is no surprise therefore to discover that the diffusion of CCTV surveillance in Europe has been more widespread in countries undergoing economic dislocation or liberalization, such as

Hungary and the UK, than it has been in "countries which have had relatively, stable welfarist-orientated governments such as Norway, Sweden, Germany and Austria" (Norris et al., 2004, p. 121). These findings are supported by more recent research on the global diffusion of open-street CCTV surveillance cameras in Brazil (Murakami Wood, 2012), Turkey (Bozbeyoglu, 2012) and South Africa (Minnaar, 2012) which reflect a broader shift in these countries away from socially progressive polices and welfare, towards exclusionary measures directed at marginalized populations. The degree of central funding committed by the state is another key factor in the global diffusion of new surveillance.

As Wacquant (2010, p. 214) points out, while the neoliberal state "embraces laissez-faire at the top", it tends to "be fiercely interventionist, bossy, and pricey" when introducing new measures to control problem populations. Thus, between 1992 and 2002 the UK central government, through its City Challenge Competition and Crime Reduction Programmes, committed over a quarter of a Billion pounds of predominantly public money to the expansion of CCTV surveillance cameras (Norris et al., 2004, p. 112). As Doyle, Lippert and Lyon (2012, p. 6) point out, "the absence of similar driving initiatives by national governments is one factor explaining the much slower dissemination of public open-street camera surveillance in other" countries[6].

4. The Politics of Surveillance in the UK: Managing Problem Populations

As indicated above, the legitimating factors behind the growth of new surveillance technologies include technological potential, the rise of the personal-information economy, risk management, national security, public perceptions, new laws and neo-liberalism (Bennett, Haggerty, Lyon, & Steeves, 2014, pp. 10-13). In their outline of the key drivers behind surveillance, Bennett et al. (2014, p. 11) define neo-liberalism as a set of "governmental policies that stress free trade and deregulated markets". However, as Wacquant (2009a, 2010) points out, neo-liberal policies include not only a preference for market rule, but also "an expansive and proactive penal apparatus", "welfare state devolution and retraction", and "the cultural trope of individual responsibility"(Wacquant, 2010, p. 197). While Wacquant used this framework to examine penal transformation in the USA, this broader sociological conception of "neo-liberalism" provides a useful conceptual framework for theorizing the emergence of new surveillance technologies in the UK crime control field. As we shall show below, the emergence of an expansive penal apparatus, welfare state retraction, and neo-liberal responsibilisation strategies are all central drivers behind the emergence of new surveillance technologies in the crime control field.

Any theory of contemporary penal change must begin by considering the wider transformation of the "field of power" ushered in by the demise of the Keynesian Welfare State (KWS) and the emergence of neo-liberalism. As a number of writers have argued, this transformation has resulted in the de-autonomization of the crime control field whereby the cultural capital of criminological and legal experts has become de-valued or de-legitimated, while political capital (in relation to crime control) has become valorised[7]. As Haggerty (2004) points out, while criminal justice policy (in the USA and UK) has always been driven by political considerations, the last two decades have seen the emergence of a more explicitly symbolic politics which values political expediency above criminological research and the emergence of a technological field of expertise which has served to "displace the policy relevance of criminology" (2004, p. 222).

Following the IRA bombings in the City of London in 1993, for example, a network of CCTV surveillance cameras was rapidly introduced to record traffic movement in and out of the city centre. Similar developments were reported after the attacks on September 11 in the United States when the "rush to surveillance" intensified further largely driven by developments in the political and journalistic fields (Ball & Webster, 2003). In this context, the introduction of new legislation or new surveillance technologies such as CCTV cameras is often announced at a political party conference or in the "journalistic field" before any systematic evaluation of their efficacy (sees Norris, 2012, p. 254). As Garland (2001) points out, the developments outlined above are also related to the demise of penal modernism which has witnessed the emergence of punitive law enforcement policies alongside risk-based strategies of social control.

For Garland (2001, pp.105-106), these developments are the result of "a new criminological predicament...the normality of high crime rates and the acknowledged limitations of the criminal justice state". The response to this predicament in the "crime control field" has resulted in a series of policies that are highly contradictory. Garland notes that on the one hand the state appears to be attempting to reclaim the power of sovereign command by the use of phrases like "zero tolerance", "prison works", and "three strikes". However, at the same time there has been an attempt to face up to the predicament and develop new pragmatic "adaptive" strategies including the "commercialization of justice" and a re-distribution of the responsibility for crime control (2001, p. 113).

While Garland (2001) sees these developments as a schizoid and disjointed response from the state to a new "criminological predicament", Wacquant (2009a, p. 301) argues that it is "a predictable organizational division in the labour of management of the disruptive poor". From this perspective, the rapid introduction of "new surveillance" technologies following highly mediatised crimes fits neatly with the "sovereign state" strategies of "denial" and "acting out" (Garland, 2001) that are manifest in the "political" and "journalistic" fields, while the emergence of actuarial regimes characterized by pre-emption, surveillance and intelligence-led policing chimes with the "adaptive strategies" (Garland, 2001) found in the penal sector of the "bureaucratic field".

As a number of writers have shown, the new surveillance practices and technologies that have been introduced in the UK is disproportionately directed to-wards those shorn of economic and cultural capital. In recent years, for example, probation policy in the UK has seen the widespread use of standardized assessment tools that are used to classify and "separate the more from the less dangerous" (Feeley & Simon, 1992, p. 452). These developments have facilitated the introduction of intensive supervision and surveillance programmes directed at "prolific" or "persistent" offenders which utilize compulsory drug testing, criminal profiling, electronic monitoring and police databases.

As Norris (2007, p. 156) has shown, the construction of this expansive surveillance apparatus in the bureaucratic field is used to monitor those shorn of capital, typically "an unemployed, drug-using male, under the age of 21, who is likely to have been in local authority care, been excluded from school and have few, if any, qualifications". Similar developments can be found in the context of "bureaucratic welfare" regimes where a plethora of new surveillance technologies have been introduced to monitor the welfare poor (Gilliom, 2001; Wacquant, 2009a). Welfare claimants in the UK and USA are surrounded by a range of surveillance technologies and programmes that intimately oversee their eligibility for work, leisure patterns and family status. In the United States, for instance, it has become increasingly difficult to distinguish the welfare office from the probation office:

Welfare offices have borrowed the stock-and-trade techniques of the correctional institution: a behaviourist philosophy of action a` la Skinner, constant close-up monitoring, strict spatial assignments and time constraints, intensive record-keeping and case management, periodic interrogation and reporting, and a rigid system of graduated sanctions for failing to perform properly (Wacquant, 2009a, p. 102).

The other central feature of neo-liberal regimes identified by Wacquant (2010) is the cultural trope of individual responsibility. In the crime control field, this involves an attempt by the state to devolve the responsibility for surveillance onto individuals and organizations. For instance, over the last two decades the CCTV Challenge Competitions and Crime Reduction Programmes devolved the responsibility for crime control in the UK on to local public-private partnerships. Moreover, empirical research in UK town centres has shown how these public-private CCTV systems can be co-opted for central state purposes and used to target "known criminals", "suspected drug addicts", and those "wanted" for the breach of bail conditions (Coleman, 2004; McCahill, 2002; Wakefield, 2003).

More recent examples of responsibilisation include the Anti Money Laundering/Counter Terrorism Financing (AML/CFT) and e-Borders surveillance regimes (Ball et al., 2015). The former requires banks and building societies to monitor customer transactions and report any suspicious activity to the Serious Organized Crime Agency, while the latter requires airlines to collect passport data in advance of travel and transfer it to the UK Border Agency for screening against watch-lists (Ball et al., 2015, p. 21). Once again these surveillance regimes do not fall equally on all populations as customer activities and financial transactions are incorporated into information infrastructures which support the identification of criminals and terrorists (Ball et al., 2015).

5. Surveillance Practice: "Habitus" and "Field"

As Ball et al. (2015) have argued, surveillance theorists have tended to provide either society-wide analysis of the emergence of a surveillance society, or micro-sociological accounts of local dynamics and resistance. However, the nature of the connection between the two levels of analysis "has not been theorised in surveillance studies in a thoroughgoing way" (2015, p. 25). The work of Bourdieu may be instructive here as his entire approach to sociology was partly an attempt to develop a new direction in social theory that would steer a course between what he considered the excessive "voluntarism" of the philosopher Jean-Paul Sartre and the excessive "structuralism" of the anthropologist Levi-Strauss. What must be explained, according to Bourdieu, "is always choice within a structured situation that individuals do not themselves consciously structure" (in Couzens Hoy, 2005, p. 119).

From this perspective, the actions and choices of individuals are shaped by "the internalization of the objective patterns of their extant social environment" (Wacquant, 2005, p. 137) and by the position they occupy in any given field. In an attempt to apply this approach to the study of penalty, Joshua Page (2013) has argued that abstract theoretical accounts of penal transformation of-ten fail to consider the intervening mechanisms that translate social-structural phenomena into penal practice. From this perspective, macro-level social trans-formations are always retranslated into the internal logic of "fields" and mediated by a field-specific "habitués" which refers to "an internal set of dispositions that shape perception, appreciation, and action" (Page, 2013, p. 152)[8]. Thus, while "macro-level, structural trends affect practice (what agents do and what decisions are made)…they do not do so automatically and without mediation" (2013, p. 154). Similar arguments can be made in relation to the crime control field. For instance, empirical research on "surveillance practice" in a range of settings has shown that despite the decline of the penal welfare model, those working within the "left hand" of the state have often opposed the measures introduced by the "right hand" of the state (Bourdieu, 1998, p. 2).

In Australia, for example, practitioners working within "welfarist" working cultures obstructed the introduction of public-space surveillance cameras (Sutton & Wilson, 2004). Similarly, research has shown how "welfare agency staff assisted clients in bettering the surveillance system" through the use of "head nods (yes) or shakes (no) as the client responded to questions during intake interviews that were logging data into the sys-tem" (Gilliom & Monahan, 2012, p. 408). At the micro-level of probation practice, meanwhile, it has been shown that the "Right hand" of the state is not always aware of what the "Left hand" is doing as "risk-based" discourses are filtered through the occupational concerns of front-line practitioners who continue to be guided by the old "welfare" mentality rather than the "risk" mentality (Kemshall & Maguire, 2001).

As the neo-liberal state attempts to devolve the responsibility for crime control, new surveillance agents have entered the crime control field bringing with them a "habitus" that shapes the way new surveillance technologies are applied in practice. For instance, empirical research on the use of CCTV surveillance camera-as in a shopping mall in Riyadh found that surveillance monitoring was filtered through the religious norms and social mores of those operating the systems. In this context, private security officers who recently left their tribal village used cameras not to target groups of "flawed consumers", but to target "singles", groups of males suspected of engaging in "courtship" behaviour in a sex-segregated society (Al-hadar & McCahill, 2011).

In the UK, ethnographic research on the operation of CCTV systems on mass private property has shown how some corporate actors continue to work with the old "welfare" mentality, empathizing with the plight of local working class youths (McCahill, 2002). One study on the use of CCTV surveillance cameras in a shopping mall situated on a deprived council estate in the north of England, reported how low paid, low status, working class security officers refused to pass on the names of "wanted" persons identified on camera to the local beat officer (McCahill, 2002).

More recently, ethnographic observations of encounters between "flawed consumers" and private security officers in an English shopping mall revealed that despite receiving "life-time" banning orders, marginalized groups utilized social capital (i.e. collusion with private security officers) to gain access to public services that were provided on private property (McCahill & Finn, 2014). Thus, while the crime control field may have changed dramatically in recent years "neither the 'culture of control' nor the 'new penology' have fully taken root in the heads and habitus of penal agents" (Page, 2013, p. 158), or in the heads of "private" actors who often find themselves monitoring their own locales and work-place situations (McCahill, 2002)[9.]

6. Surveillance, Capital and Resistance

One of Bourdieu's central contributions to social theory was to demonstrate that it is not only "economic capital" (i.e. money or property) that functions as a determinant of social position, but also "social capital" in the form of networks and social relationships, "cultural capital" such as education, skills and cultural knowledge, and "symbolic capital" which designates the authority, knowledge, prestige, or reputation that an individual or group has accumulated (Bourdieu, 1986). While previous research has shown how these forms of capital can be mobilized by the institutional actors conducting surveillance (Dupont, 2004, p. 244), this section draws upon ethnographic research to show how the subjective experience and response to surveillance is also shaped by the distribution of capitals (see McCahill & Finn, 2014).

For instance, our research has shown that relatively privileged groups, such as "middle class" protesters or police officers, utilized economic, social and cultural capital to evade or contest surveillance in various ways. Protesters utilized social capital (e.g. personal contacts with senior police officers, lawyers, MPs, local councilors, journalists, and associates working in the "privacy" movement) and cultural capital (e.g. knowledge of the law) to challenge surveillance through the courts, or to discover the "fate of their data" through Freedom of Information re-quests. Similarly, police officers and security officers working under the gaze of CCTV surveillance cameras utilized social and cultural capital to manage not just when they appeared on CCTV, but also how they appeared on camera.

In this case, knowledge of either operating the systems or visiting control rooms enabled plural police actors to avoid the gaze of surveillance camera operators by locating themselves in "blind spots" when patrolling the shopping malls or streets. Alternatively, plural police actors would visit surveillance camera control rooms to review footage, reflect on their bodily comportment, and modify their behaviour in future "face-to-face" interactions (McCa-hill & Finn, 2014).

However, it is not only relatively privileged groups who utilize capitals to contest surveillance in various ways. As Bennett et al. (2010, p. 29) have suggested, "rather than assume an essential unity to cultural capital", it may be useful to explore how other forms of cultural know-how may serve to function "as sources of cultural privilege" in a range of new settings and situations. For instance, in his later work Bourdieu (2005) used the concept of "technical capital" "to refer to the distinctive assets that members of the working classes acquire through their vocational skills and pass on to their children through domestic training" (in Bennett et al., 2010, p. 29).

Bourdieu (1990) also referred to the "lucidity of the excluded" to illustrate how the exclusion of marginalized groups from certain realms of privilege can often accord them a certain critical insight in-to the structures that oppress them (see McNay, 2000). Thus, alongside the "master" concepts of capital identified by Bourdieu, we have introduced the term surveillance capital to explain how surveillance subjects utilize the everyday forms of tacit knowledge that is acquired through first-hand experience of power relations to challenge the very same power relations. For instance, our ethnographic research showed how "prolific" offenders were aware that probation officers shared information with other agencies because of what they had read on the induction forms that they were required to sign. Others were aware that any in-formation they might give away during interviews was likely to be stored on the database. One prolific of-fender summed it up when he said: "Like the police that work with me make out that they're not the police and they work with probation and that, but they're full on undercover coppers. The quicker you get to learn that the better inn it? You don't want to be an idiot and pretend that they're not proper police (in McCahill & Finn, 2014)".

Moreover, while the information stored on databases can be treated as the source of "truth" that overrides personal testimonies, some "prolific" offenders used the existence of the "file" or "database" to avoid "opening up" and answering questions during face-to-face interviews by telling drugs workers in the probation office to "go check the file". "Prolific" offenders al-so used the existence of "new technologies" to evade monitoring by keeping text messages sent by the probation staff to prove that they had not missed or were not late for appointments.

One "prolific" offender used the data that had been extracted from his body to his advantage when he requested photo-copies of any "negative" drug tests to take home and show his partner that he was not using drugs. Family members of "prolific" offenders also used surveillance against surveillance to support their case when confronted by the police. One mother kept fragments of her son's "digital persona" (electronically-recorded consumer transactions) to challenge police decisions to question or arrest her son. While surveillance capital may not be easily translated into other forms of "capital", it does provide surveillance subjects with a degree of agency in local and specific settings.

As Bourdieu argued, while "those who dominate in a given field are in a position to make it function to their advantage...they must always contend with the resistance, the claims, the contention...of the dominated" (Bourdieu & Wacquant, 1992, p. 102). However, the French author was also well aware of the ironies of resistance and the potential for these strategies to re-produce existing social divisions. In an attempt to conceptualize these issues, he used "the term 'regulated liberties' to denote a more complex relation between the dominant and its subjects" (Bourdieu, 1990, p. 102). Here Bourdieu (1990) drew attention to what he described as "the un-resolvable contradiction of resistance", whereby the dominated "can resist by trying to efface the signs of difference that have led to their domination", or they can "dominate their own domination by accepting and accentuating the characteristics that mark them as dominated" (in Couzens Hoy, 2005, p. 135).

In recent years, a number of writers have drawn upon these ideas to explore the relationship between surveillance, body capital and class divisions following the shift from an industrial society organised around manufacturing and heavy industry to a post-industrial society dominated by the service sector and consumerism. In the field of employment the decline of heavy industry which valued a "type of 'body capital' forged through notions of physical hardness and a patriarchal breadwinner", now seems out of step in a consumer or service economy "that values flexibility, keyboard proficiency, telephone communication skills and personal presentation" (Nayak, 2006, p. 817). The exclusion of working class males from the field of employment in post-industrial cities is compounded by exclusion from public spaces due to embodied attributes which are considered "out of place" in the new spaces of consumption. Nayak (2006, p. 821) for example has shown how the "body capital" of young working males in Newcastle led to their exclusion from clubs and bars in the city centre.

He refers to how so-called "charvers" "hold their head" and "arch their backs when walking". The targeting practices of open-street CCTV operators in UK cities are also said to fall disproportionately on those who look "too confident for their own good" or who had their "head up, back straight, upper body moving too much", or those who were "swaggering, looking hard" (Norris & Armstrong, 1999, p. 122). In our ethnographic account of the subjective experience of surveillance in a northern city in the UK, we showed how marginalized groups responded to CCTV monitoring by covering their faces with hats and scarves, flicking "V signs" at surveillance camera operators, and throwing bricks at cameras. Of course, those who obscure their faces with clothing or who oriented their behaviour to camera operators through confrontation and abusive gestures are often singled out for further attention by surveillance camera operators (see Norris, 2003, p. 265). In this context, the body becomes both a "performance" and a "straitjacket" (Shilling, 2003) as the "bodily hexis" (dialect, accent, dress, body posture and demeanour) conveys resistant impressions that potentially leads to further surveillance and exclusion (McCahill & Finn, 2014).

7. Conclusion

The surveillance studies literature has been dominated by Foucaultian and Deleuzian-inspired perspectives on "discipline" (Foucault, 1977) and "control" (Deleuze, 1992). The aim of this paper has not been to "go be-yond" Foucault or Deleuze. The work produced by these towering intellectuals is far too important for that and will no doubt continue to frame theoretical debates on surveillance for decades to come. Instead, our aims were much more modest and were simply to propose an alternative approach to the study of surveillance that replaced a discursive analysis of historical texts with empirically-informed "field" theory. As Haggerty (2006, pp. 41-42) argues, while surveillance theorists might want to embrace many of Foucault's insights, they may also want to reserve "space for modestly realist projects that analyze the politics of surveillance or the experiences of the subjects of surveillance".

To do this, we argued, required a different approach to Foucault whose main concern was with the forms that power relations take and "the techniques they depend upon, rather than upon the groups and individuals who dominate or are dominated as a consequence" (Luke, 2005, p. 89). As Foucault (2001, p. 331) explained, "the main objective of struggles is to attack not so much such-or-such institution of power, or group, or elite, or class but, rather, a technique, a form of power". Thus, whereas Foucault begins with an "'ascending analysis of power starting from its infinitesimal mechanisms', Bourdieu gives priority to a focused analysis of the nexus of institutions that ensures the reproduction of economic and cultural capital" in the wider field of power (Wacquant, 2005, p. 145).

Drawing upon this approach, we argued that the demise of the Keynesian Welfare State (KWS) and the rise of neo-liberal economic policies in the UK has Media and Communication, 2015, Volume 3, Issue 2, Pages 10-20 18 placed new surveillance technologies at the centre of a reconfigured "crime control field" (Garland, 2001) de-signed to control the problem populations created by neo-liberal economic policies (Wacquant, 2009a). At the same time, however, we suggested that field theory offers the potential to examine national variations in the up-take of new surveillance technologies by showing how globalizing forces and wider social changes are filtered through the political and juridical fields of different national jurisdictions. This approach also provides a bridge between society-wide analysis and micro-sociology by showing how surveillance practice is filtered through the existing organizational, occupational and individual concerns of surveillance agents.

Following this, we situated the introduction of new surveillance within "fields of struggle", arguing that the distribution of various forms of "capital"—economic, social, cultural and symbolic—operate as a range of goods or resources that structure the dynamics of surveillance practices and power relations in the crime control field. In this respect, our analysis involved a critical engagement with two theoretical traditions–Focaultian approaches which provide dystopian visions of the power of state surveillance while under-playing agency, and integrationist perspectives on the "everyday politics of resistance" (Marx, 2002; J. C. Scott, 1990) which often fail to consider how "the interaction itself owes its form to the objective structures which have produced the dispositions of the interacting agents and which allot them their relative positions in the interaction and elsewhere" (Bourdieu, 1977, p. 81).

To sum up therefore we have attempted to combine a macro-level analysis which explores how globalizing forces are filtered through the "field of power" in different national jurisdictions, with a micro-level analysis which shows how new surveillance measures are mediated by the "habitus" of surveillance agents and surveillance subjects. This approach, we argue, advances our understanding of surveillance politics in two ways. First, it can "act as solvent of the new neoliberal common sense that 'naturalizes' the current state of affairs" (Wacquant, 2009b, p. 129) by demonstrating that there are alternatives to the "bad example" set by neo-liberal countries such as the UK where the "processes of normalization of surveillance have gone much further than elsewhere" (Murakami Wood & Webster, 2009, p. 260). Second, it provides a corrective to "top-down" surveillance theories which continue to portray surveillance subjects as "docile bodies", rather than social actors who can contest power relations in a field that is very much skewed against them.

COGITATIO: Media and Communication (ISSN: 2183-2439) 2015, Volume 3, Issue 2, Pages 10-20 Doi: 10.17645/mac.v3i2.251, Michael McCahill's research focuses on the social impact of "new surveillance" technologies in the context of policing and criminal justice. This article is licensed under a Creative Commons Attribution 4.0 International License (CC BY). Theorizing Surveillance in the UK Crime Control Field. Michael McCahill: School of Social Science, University of Hull, Hull, UK; 30 September 2015

Chapter 7

Artificial Intelligence Governance and Ethics: Global Perspectives

*Angela Daly, Thilo Hagendorff, Li Hui,
Monique Mann, Vidushi Marda, Ben Wagner,
Wei Wang and Saskia Witteborn*

1 Introduction

Artificial intelligence (AI) is a technology which is increasingly being utilized in society and the economy worldwide, and its implementation is planned to become more prevalent in coming years. AI is increasingly being embedded in our lives, supplementing our pervasive use of digital technologies. But this is being accompanied by disquiet over problematic and dangerous implementations of AI, or indeed, even AI itself deciding to do dangerous and problematic actions, especially in fields such as the military, medicine and criminal justice. These developments have led to concerns about whether and how AI systems adhere, and will adhere to ethical standards. These concerns have stimulated a global conversation on AI ethics, and have resulted in various actors from different countries and sectors issuing ethics and governance initiatives and guidelines for AI. Such developments form the basis for our research in this report, combining our international and interdisciplinary expertise to give an insight into what is happening in Australia, China, Europe, India and the US.

What is AI?

Artificial Intelligence (AI) is an emerging area of computer science. There are numerous definitions and various terms used interchangeably to describe 'AI' within the academic literature (and also popular discourse)-these include, for example: algorithmic, or profiling, automation, (supervised/unsupervised) machine learning, deep neural networks etc. In general terms, AI could be defined as technology that automatically detects patterns in data, and makes predictions on the basis of them. It is a method of inferential analysis that identifies correlations within datasets that can, in the case of profiling, be used as an indicator to classify a subject as a representative of a category or group (Hildebrandt 2008; Schreurs et al 2008). A broad distinction is made between 'narrow' and 'general' or 'broad' AI. Narrow AI is an AI application which is designed to deal with one particular task and reflects most currently existing applications of AI in daily life, while general or broad AI reflects human intelligence in its versatility to handle different or general tasks. In this report when we discuss AI we refer to AI in its narrow form.

There are numerous applications of AI in a range of domains, perhaps contributing to definitional complexity, for example, predictive analytics (such as recidivism prediction in criminal justice contexts, predictive policing, forecasting risk in business and finance), automated identification via facial recognition etc. Indeed, AI has been deployed in a range of contexts and social domains, with mixed outcomes, including insurance, finance, education, employment, marketing, governance, security, and policing (see e.g., O'Neil 2016; Ferguson 2017).

AI and Ethics

At this relatively early stage in AI's development and implementation, the issue has arisen of AI adhering to certain ethical principles (see e.g. Arkin 2009; Mason 2017), and the ability of existing laws to govern AI has emerged as key as to how future AI will be developed, deployed and implemented (see e.g. Leenes & Lucivero 2015; Calo 2015; Wachter et al. 2017a).

While originally confined to theoretical, technical and academic debates, the issue of governing AI has recently entered the mainstream with both governments and private companies from major geopolitical powers including the US, China, European Union and India formulating statements and policies regarding AI and ethics (see e.g. European Commission 2018; Pichai 2018). A key issue here is precisely what are the ethical standards to which AI should adhere? Furthermore, the transnational nature of digitised technologies, the key role of private corporations in AI development and implementation and the globalised economy gives rise to questions about which jurisdictions/actors will decide on the legal and ethical standards to which AI may adhere, and whether we may end up with a 'might is right' approach where it is these large geopolitical players which set the agenda for AI regulation and ethics for the whole world.

Further questions arise around the enforceability of ethics statements regarding AI, both in terms of whether they reflect existing fundamental legal principles and are legally enforceable in specific jurisdictions, and also the extent to which the principles can be operationalised and integrated into AI systems and application in practice.

What does 'ethics' mean in AI?

Ethics is seen as a reflection theory of morality or as the theory of the good life. A distinction can be made between fundamental ethics, which is concerned with abstract moral principles, and applied ethics (Höffe 2013). The latter also includes ethics of technology, which contains in turn AI ethics as a subcategory. Roughly speaking, AI ethics serves for the self-reflection of computer and engineering sciences, which are engaged in the research and development of AI or machine learning. In this context, dynamics such as individual technology development projects, or the development of new technologies as a whole, can be analyzed. Likewise, causal mechanisms and functions of certain technologies can be investigated using a more static analysis (Rahwan et al. 2019). Typical topics are self-driving cars, political manipulation by AI applications, autonomous weapon systems, facial recognition, algorithmic discrimination, conversational bots, and social sorting by ranking algorithms, and many more (Hagendorff 2019).

Key demands of AI ethics relate to aspects such as the reflection of research goals and purposes, the direction of research funding, the linkage between science and politics, the security of AI systems, the responsibility links underlying the development and use of AI technologies, the inscription of values in technical artefacts, the orientation of the technology sector towards the common good, and much more (Future of Life Institute 2017).

Last but not least, AI ethics is also reflected within the framework of meta-ethics, in which questions about the effectiveness of normative demands are investigated. Ethical discourses can either be held with close proximity to their designated object, or it can be the opposite. The advantage of a close proximity is that those ethical discourses can have a concrete impact on the course of action in a particular organization dealing with AI. The downside is that this kind of ethical reflection has to be quite narrow and pragmatic. Uttering more radical demands only makes only sense when ethical discourses have a certain distance to their designated object. Nevertheless, those ethical discourses are typically rather inefficient and have hardly any effect in practice.

Another dimension of AI ethics concerns the degree of its normatively. Here, ethics can oscillate between irritation and orientation. Irritation equals weak normatively. This means an abstinence from strong normative claims. Instead, ethics just uncovers blind spots or describes hitherto underrepresented issues. Orientation, on the other hand, means strong normatively. The downside of making strong normative claims is that they provoke backfire or boomerang-effects, meaning that people tend to react to perceived external constraints on action with that kind of behavior they are supposed to refrain from. Therefore, AI ethics must satisfy two traits in order to be effective. First, it should use weak normatively and should not universally determine what is right and what is wrong. Second, AI ethics should seek close proximity to its designated object. This implies that ethics is understood as an inter or trans-disciplinary field of study, that is directly linked to the adjacent computer sciences or industry organizations, and that is active within these fields.

This Report

In this Report we combine our interdisciplinary and international expertise as researchers working on AI policy, ethics and governance to give an overview of some of our countries and regions' approaches to the topic of AI and ethics. We do not claim to present an exhaustive account of approaches to this issue internationally, but we do aim to give a snapshot of how some countries and regions, especially 'large' ones like China, Europe, India and the United States are, or are not, addressing the topic. We also include some initiatives at national level of EU Member States (Germany, Austria and the United Kingdom) and initiatives in Australia, all of which can be considered 'smaller'. The selection of these countries and regions has been driven by our own familiarity with them from prior experience. We acknowledge the limitations of our approach that we do not have contributions regarding this issue from Africa, Latin America, the Middle East, Russia, Indigenous views of AI and AI and ethics approaches informed by religious beliefs (see e.g. Cisse 2018; ELRC 2019; Indigenous AI n.d.). In future work we hope to be able to cover more countries and approaches to AI ethics.

We have specifically looked to government, corporate and some other initiatives which frame and situate themselves in the realm of 'AI governance' or 'AI ethics'. We acknowledge that other initiatives, such as those relevant to 'big data' and the 'Internet of Things' may also be relevant to AI governance and ethics; but with a few exceptions, these are beyond the scope of this report. Further work should be done on 'connecting the dots' between some predecessor digital technology governance initiatives and the current drive for AI ethics and governance. The fast-moving nature of this topic and field is our reason for publishing this report in this current form. We hope the report is useful and illuminating for readers. We welcome comments and other feedback on the work to date, and expressions of interest in future collaboration with us on this and related topics.

2. Global Level

International organizations

At the international level, the most prominent AI ethics guidelines are the recently-released OECD Principles on AI (2019). The OECD is an international economic organization of 36 Member States, mostly comprising high-income economies. The Principles have been endorsed by, among others, the US Trump Administration (Pressman & Lashinsky 2019), and six non-member states (Argentina, Brazil, Colombia, Costa Rica, Peru and Romania). In June 2019 ministers from the Group of 20 (G20) major economies agreed on a set of guiding principles for using AI, which are derived from the aforementioned OECD Principles, but are also characterized as non-binding (G20 2019). Notably, China and Russia are G20 countries but not OECD members (Koizumi 2019).

There are various activities that the United Nations (UN) and its constituent bodies are undertaking which relate to AI (ITU 2018). While at the time of writing the UN and its constituent bodies have not issued their own ethics or governance principles on AI, UNICEF and the United Nations Development Program (UNDP) are members of the multi-stakeholder Partnership on AI (discussed below). UNESCO is also working on a possible 'normative instrument' on the topic (ITU 2018). The United Nations Interregional Crime and Justice Research Institute is in the process of opening a Centre for Artificial Intelligence and Robotics in The Hague, Netherlands. An attempt in 2018 to open formal negotiations to reform the UN Convention on Certain Conventional Weapons to govern or prohibit fully autonomous lethal weapons were blocked by the US and Russia, among others (Delcker 2018).

The Council of Europe has also been active on the topic of AI. These developments are included in the next section on Europe.

At the 40th International Conference of Data Protection & Privacy Commissioners (ICDPPC) in 2018, which took place in

Brussels, a Declaration on Ethics and Data Protection in Artificial Intelligence was released by delegates from various national data protection and privacy authorities. The Declaration sets out six guiding principles and calls for 'common governance principles on artificial intelligence' to be established. The ICDPPC has also set up a permanent working group on Ethics and Data Protection in Artificial Intelligence.

Technical initiatives

The most prominent initiative from the technical community can be found in the IEEE's work on AI, in the form of its Global Initiative on Ethics of Autonomous and Intelligent Systems. The IEEE (Institute of Electrical and Electronic Engineers) has involved its membership of technical experts, but also reached beyond to non-IEEE members to participate in this project. The initiative has produced two versions to date of Ethically Aligned Design, involving 'hundreds of participants over six continents' (IEEE 2018). Version 2 includes five General Principles to guide the ethical design, development and implementation of autonomous and intelligent systems. In line with IEEE's general activities, the development of technical standards based on these discussions on ethics is envisaged by the Global Initiative, and a series of working groups have been set up under the Global Initiative to work towards this goal.

Global multi-stakeholder initiatives

Some multinational corporations have also released their own ethics statements. Since many of these corporations originate in the US, they are included later in the section on the US. There is one group which may be considered truly global, and also multi-stakeholder in its membership, namely the Partnership on AI. As mentioned, some UN agencies are among its members, as well as NGOs (such as Article 19), academic research institutes (such as the Australian National University 3Ai Centre), public sector agencies (including the BBC) and also technology firms such as Amazon but also Chinese giant Baidu. The Partnership on AI has released its 8 'Tenets' (Partnership on AI n.d.).

The World Economic Forum, funded by its member corporations from around the world, has commenced various activities on AI, principally through its Centre for the Fourth Industrial Revolution in San Francisco (US). Part of this Centre's work is to co-design and pilot policy and governance frameworks including for AI with governments and corporations. In 2019 the WEF released a White Paper on the topic of AI governance.

3 Europe

In this section some AI governance and ethics initiatives which have been developed in Europe will be outlined. These include developments by the European Union (EU), Council of Europe (CoE) and in some individual nations (which happen to be members of both the EU and CoE).

European Union

The EU has been positioning itself as a frontrunner in the global debate on AI governance and ethics. A major piece of legislation, the General Data Protection Regulation (GDPR) came into effect in 2018, and has a scope which extends to some organizations outside of the EU in certain circumstances. Of direct interest for AI governance are the provisions contained in Section 5 of the GDPR on the Right to Object (Article 21) and Automated Individual Decision-Making Including Profiling (Article 22). There is significant discussion as to precisely what these provisions entail in practice regarding algorithmic decision-making, automation and profiling and whether they are adequate to address the concerns that arise from such processes (see e.g. Edwards & Veale 2017; Wachter, Mittelstadt & Floridi 2017b).

Among other prominent developments in the EU is the European Parliament Resolution on Civil Law Rules on Robotics from February 2017. While the Resolution is not binding, it expresses the Parliament's opinion, and makes various requests of the European Commission to carry out further work on the topic. In particular, the Resolution 'consider[ed] that the existing Union legal framework should be updated and complemented, where appropriate, by guiding ethical principles in line with the complexity of robotics and its many social, medical and bioethical implications' and set out in its Annex a proposed Code of Ethical Conduct for Robotics Engineers, Code for Research Ethics Committees, Licence for Designers and License for Users. The Parliament also requested the European Commission to submit a 'proposal for a legislative instrument on legal questions related to the development and use of robotics and AI foreseeable in the next 10 to 15 years, combined with non-legislative instruments such as guidelines and codes of conduct as referred to in recommendations set out in the Annex'. At the time of writing, the Commission has not yet released such a proposal.

Further initiatives have occurred subsequent to this European Parliament Resolution. In March 2018, the European Commission issued a Communication on Artificial Intelligence for Europe, in which the Commission set out 'a European initiative on AI' with three main aims: of boosting the EU's technological and industrial capacity, and AI uptake; of preparing for socio-economic changes brought about by AI (with a focus on labour, social security and education); and of ensuring 'an appropriate ethical and legal framework, based on the Union's values and in line with the Charter of Fundamental Rights of the EU'. Also in March 2018, the European Group on Ethics in Science and New Technologies, an independent advisory body to the President of the European Commission comprising interdisciplinary experts, released its Statement on Artificial Intelligence, Robotics and Autonomous Systems. The Statement proposed 'a set of basic principles and democratic prerequisites, based on the fundamental values laid down in the EU Treaties and in the EU Charter of Fundamental Rights'.

Most prominent of the EU initiatives has been the European Union High-Level Expert Group on Artificial Intelligence (a multi-stakeholder group of 52 experts from academia, civil society and industry) finalizing its Ethics Guidelines for Trustworthy AI in April 2019 (2019a). They include 7 key, but non-exhaustive, requirements that AI systems should meet in order to be 'trustworthy'. The requirements will go through a 'piloting process' whereby they will be tested in private and public sector organization, with feedback sought to inform a public document scheduled for release in early 2020.

A member of the High-Level Expert Group, Thomas Metzinger, criticised the process and output as 'ethics washing' in an op-ed for German newspaper Der Tagesspeigel in 2019. In particular he pointed to the removal of 'red line' 'non-negotiable' text from the final version of the Guidelines as an example of this, and called for academia and civil society to take charge of the discussion on AI governance and ethics, especially away from industry. Nevertheless, Metzinger still considers that the ethics guidelines produced by the Group are 'the best in the world' especially as compared to efforts from the US and China.

This 'first deliverable' of the High-Level Expert Group was followed by their 'second deliverable', Policy and Investment Recommendations for Trustworthy AI in June 2019 (2019b). The document contains 33 recommendations 'that can guide Trustworthy AI towards sustainability, growth and competitiveness, as well as inclusion–while empowering, benefiting and protecting human beings'. Among the recommendations, along with ones pertaining to education, research, government use of AI and investment priorities, is strong criticism of both state and corporate surveillance using AI, including that governments should commit not to engage in mass surveillance and the commercial surveillance of individuals including via 'free' services should be countered. This is furthered by a specific recommendation that AI-enabled 'mass scoring' of individuals be banned. The Panel also recommends that sustainability be taken account of, including the enactment of a circular economy plan for digital technologies and AI. The Panel calls for more work to be done to assess existing legal and regulatory frameworks to discern whether they are adequate to address the Panel's recommendations or whether reform is necessary in order to do so, with particular regard being paid to: the monitoring and restriction of automated lethal weapons; the monitoring of personalized AI systems built on children's profiles; and the monitoring of AI systems used in the private sector which significantly impact on human lives, with the possibility of introducing further obligations on such providers.

The language of 'red lines' is included in this document, and as mentioned above, the Panel expresses concern with some particular uses of AI, including examples it believes should be prohibited. This may stymie some of the previous criticism regarding the Guidelines being 'ethics washing' but it is still significant that that language was excluded from the Guidelines even if it has ended up in the Recommendations. Furthermore, it is unclear to what extent the Panel's Recommendations will actually be followed by EU institutions and put into practice in reality.

Council of Europe

The Council of Europe (CoE), which includes all EU Member States as well as additional non-EU members in Eastern Europe, Turkey and Russia, has also been active on the topic of AI. Of these activities, there are two which directly relate to AI governance and ethics. The first is the European Commission for the Efficiency of Justice (CEPEJ) European Ethical Charter on the use of artificial intelligence (AI) in judicial systems and their environment, adopted in December 2018, which contains five principles to guide the development of AI tools in European judiciaries. The European Committee on Legal Co-operation (CDCJ) is at the time of writing working on draft guidelines for policymakers designing online dispute resolution systems (ODRs) to ensure compatibility with the right to a fair trial and the right to an effective remedy under the European Convention on Human Rights. These guidelines are projected to be released in late 2020.

The second notable CoE activity is the Guidelines on Artificial Intelligence and Data Protection published by the Consultative Committee of the Convention for the Protection of Individuals with regard to Automatic Processing of Personal Data (Convention 108) in January 2019. This follows Guidelines on Big Data issued in 2017, and the modernization of Convention 108 which included additions to address algorithmic decision-making. Convention 108 includes among its signatories some non-CoE members including Mauritius, Mexico and Senegal.

Germany

As a consequence of the significant financial support Germany is giving to AI research, a national 'AI Strategy' has been published (Bundesministerium für Bildung und Forschung et al 2018). The aims of the initiative are to strengthen Germany as a research location and to support the domestic economy. Just to give one example, between Tuebingen and Stuttgart the so-called 'Cyber Valley' is supposed to become one of the world's leading research locations for AI as a 'key technology'. The state government, companies, universities and other research institutions are cooperating in this project. The high monetary expenditure for AI research – the Federal Government will spend €500 million as a first step and €3 billion altogether – is justified almost exclusively with reference to the aim of survival in international competition or at least not wanting to fall behind, especially the US and China. According to the strategy, Germany is to become one of the 'world's leading locations for AI'.

Within the competitive relationships with other countries, Germany – in accordance with the principles of the EU Strategy for Artificial Intelligence (Pekka et al 2018) – intends to position itself in such a way that it sets itself apart from other, non-European nations through data protection-friendly, trustworthy, and 'human centered' AI systems, which are supposed to be used for the common good as well as for 'lighthouse applications' in the fields of climate and environment protection. At the centre of these claims is the establishment of the 'Artificial Intelligence Made in Germany' brand, which is supposed to become a globally acknowledged label of quality.

Part of this 'brand' is the idea that AI applications made in Germany, or, to be more precise, the datasets these AI applications use stand under the umbrella of data sovereignty, informational self-determination and data safety. Moreover, to ensure that AI research and innovation is in line with ethical and legal standards a Data Ethics Commission was founded, which is able to recommendations to the Federal Government and to give advice on how to use AI in an ethically sound manner. The crucial question, however, is whether the tenets of AI ethics are implemented into practice effectively.

The federal government's strategy is to create one hundred new professorships in AI and Machine Learning. A total of twelve agglomerations for research and innovation are to be established. It is hoped that this will attract excellent researchers from abroad. Furthermore, it is intended that close cooperation with France will result in competitive advantages in research and industry. In addition, there is a special focus on the promotion of medium-sized enterprises. Further fields of action include the promotion of procedures to facilitate the auditing and interpretability of algorithmic prediction and decision-making systems as well as AI safety. Overall, it can be stated that Germany has a clear national 'roadmap' for the promotion and use of AI technologies.

Austria

AI is viewed in Austria as offering a considerable competitive advantage to the nation. Drafting on an 'Artificial Intelligence Mission Austria 2030' was started, which has included a long list of stakeholder meetings to ensure participation of all relevant actors. While both participation methods used and stakeholder selection have not always been ideal, the initiative does represent at least an attempt to co-develop an Austrian AI strategy with hundreds of stakeholders. Its focus on the year 2030 is also evidently modelled on China's New Generation Artificial Intelligence Development Plan 2030 strategy, and like many similar European initiatives can be seen in response to China's position in the race to dominate the field of AI.

Austria has also shown a strong interest in European collaboration in this area, attempting to ensure that a frequently debated European 'Algorithms Rating Agency' or 'AI Ethics Authority'-modeled on the IAEA that is being currently being discussed in European policy circles-is eventually located in Vienna. Austria is the seat of numerous relevant international organizations such as the UN bodies, OSCE or the IAEA and sees such an authority as a natural continuation of its existing role in this area. At the same time members of the Austrian government have openly expressed interest in creating a large national data pool, whereby Austrian citizens' data would be sold to the highest bidder in order to attract cutting edge data-driven research to Austria. Despite evident conflict with the GDPR and other existing data protection rules, this idea remains popular in relevant policy circles.

It all stems from the acknowledgement that Austria knows that it is a small country and thus cannot compete at a global level in all domains. The data-pooling strategy is thus seen as a key competitive advantage to ensure that Austria is able to compete in a competitive international environment as a small country. Due to the disintegration of the Austrian government as part of the 'Ibiza scandal' in May 2019 - involving a video featuring political bribes, a table of what looks like cocaine and attacks on political attacks on leading Austrian newspapers by the far right-wing FPÖ party - it is unclear how and even whether the Artificial Intelligence Mission Austria 2030 will continue. However, it is to be assumed that some version of this strategy will be implemented in the coming years, regardless of which government is in power.

United Kingdom

The UK Government has linked AI development directly to its industrial strategy, and also seems to view this as giving the UK a potential competitive edge, particularly in the current context of the UK leaving the EU, or 'Brexit', and uncertainty as to what kind of political, economic and social future may lie for the UK subsequent to this point. In its 2017 Industrial Strategy, the UK Government identified 'putting the UK at the forefront of the artificial intelligence and data revolution' as one of four 'Grand Challenges' for the country, adding that it would invest in business, research and education in the UK to meet the challenge, including an AI Sector Deal which was commenced in 2018. The UK government also proclaimed its vision that the UK 'will lead the world in safe and ethical use of data and artificial intelligence giving confidence and clarity to citizens and business', including by setting up a Centre for Data Ethics and Innovation as an advisory body to this effect in what the Government claims is a 'world first' (although this seems very similar to Germany's approach detailed above). The Centre has since been set up but has not produced any substantive outputs at the time of writing. As regards international governance, the Government asserted in its Industrial Strategy that it would be an 'active participant' in standard setting and regulatory bodies especially for AI and data protection.

The UK Parliament has also been active in its consideration of AI governance and ethics issues. An All-Party Parliamentary Group on AI was set up in 2017; and a Select Committee on AI was also formed to investigate the topic, seek input from interested stakeholders and then issued a report in 2018. The Select Committee's report (re)asserted the UK's place among the 'best countries in the world for researchers and businesses developing AI' but acknowledged that the UK may be unable to compete with the size of investments in AI being made by China and the US - although it could find better comparisons in the form of Canada and Germany. The UK could draw on what was perceived as its existing strengths and position itself as a leader in the ethical development of AI.

The Select Committee did not consider that it was necessary to introduce AI-specific regulation at this point in time, but advocated for further work to be done assessing whether additions to existing legal and regulatory frameworks to deal with AI may be necessary in the future. The Select Committee did advance 5 non-legally binding 'overarching principles', as the basis for a possible cross-sector 'AI Code' that it suggested be formulated and developed by the Centre for Data Ethics and Innovation. Finally of relevance here is the Select Committee's recommendation to the UK Government to convene a 'global summit' by the end of 2019 involving different stakeholder groups to 'develop a common framework for the ethical development and deployment of artificial intelligence systems' which 'should be aligned with existing international governance structures'. It is unclear whether such an event will indeed be organised by the end of 2019.

In addition, the UK Government was the first government to partner with the World Economic Forum's aforementioned Centre for the Fourth Industrial Revolution in its project to co-design guidelines for the public procurement of AI products and services for public sector uses (Russo 2018). At the time of writing, this work is underway, but no outputs have yet been produced.

Clouding the picture for the UK, in AI and other matters, is its pending departure from the European Union and the uncertainty about what the post-EU future holds for the country. The UK Government's activities in this area have been criticized by some stakeholder groups for not investing enough compared to other Western European countries and also making 'wrong' investments (Walker 2018). In addition, EU investment in AI and robotics will likely be no longer available for research and development in the UK, which to date has been a major recipient of these funds (Walker 2018). The EU also seems to be forging ahead of domestic UK initiatives regarding ethical AI development, which also may call into question how successful the desire to be a world leader, especially in ethical AI development, will be for the UK in a post-Brexit future.

4. India

India's approach to AI is substantially informed by three initiatives at the national level. The first is Digital India, which aims to make India a digitally empowered knowledge economy. The second is making in India, under which the Government of India is prioritising AI technology designed and developed in India, and the third is the Smart Cities Mission (Marda 2018). Alongside this, there is significant investment towards research, development and training in emerging technologies in particular from the Union Government. An AI Task Force constituted by the Ministry of Commerce and Industry in 2017 looked at AI as a socio-economic problem solver at scale. In its Report (Government of India Ministry of Commerce and Industry 2018) it identified 10 key sectors in which AI should be deployed, including national security, financial technology, manufacturing and agriculture, among others. Similarly, a National Strategy for Artificial Intelligence was published in 2018 (Niti Aayog 2018) that went further to look at AI as a lever for economic growth, social development, and considers India as a potential 'garage' for AI applications. While ethics are mentioned in both documents, they fail to meaningfully engage with issues of fundamental rights, fairness, inclusion, and the limits of data driven decision making. These are also heavily influenced by the private sector, with civil society and academia, rarely, if ever, being invited into these discussions.

AI is being used in various sectors by private actors - from manufacturing, to healthcare, to finance. Notwithstanding encouraging developments, the current absence of data protection legislation in India raises crucial questions for how sensitive personal data is currently processed and shared. The current Personal Data Protection bill also fails to adequately engage with the question of inferred data, which is particularly important in the context of machine learning. India's biometric identity project, Aadhaar, could also potentially become central point of AI applications in the future, with a few proposals for use of facial recognition in the last year, although that is not the case currently. There is no ethical framework or principles published by the Government at the time of writing. It is likely that ethical principles will emerge shortly, following public attention on data protection law. Current references to AI are often in the context of data protection law, which is an increasing trend across jurisdictions.

5. China

Along with the EU, of the 'large jurisdictions' under consideration in this paper, China is the other one which has generated the most state-supported or -led AI governance and ethics initiatives.

In 2017 China's State Council issued The New-Generation AI Development Plan, which advanced China's objective of high investment in the AI sector in the coming years, and aim of becoming the world leader in AI innovation (FLIA 2017). An interim goal, by 2025, is to formulate new laws and regulations, and ethical norms and policies related to AI development in China. This includes participation in international standard setting, or even 'taking the lead' in such activities as well as 'deepen[ing] international cooperation in AI laws and regulations'.

Subsequent to this have been further initiatives on AI ethics and governance. In May 2019, the Beijing AI Principles were released by the Beijing Academy of Artificial Intelligence, which depicted the core of its AI development as 'the realization of beneficial AI for humankind and nature'. In addition, the Principles considered:

- the risk of human unemployment by encouraging more research on Human-AI coordination;

- avoiding the negative implications of 'malicious AI race' by promoting cooperation, also on a global level;

- integrating AI policy with its rapid development in a dynamic and responsive way by making special guidelines across sectors; and

- continuously making preventive and forecasting policy in a long-term perspective with respect to risks posed by Augmented Intelligence, Artificial General Intelligence (AGI) and Super intelligence. The Principles have been supported by various elite Chinese universities and companies including Baidu, Alibaba and Tencent.

Another group comprising top Chinese universities and companies and led by the Ministry of Industry and Information Technology (MIIT)'s China Academy of Information and Communications Technology, the Artificial Intelligence Industry Alliance (AIIA), released its Joint Pledge on Self Discipline in the Artificial Intelligence Industry, also in May 2019 (Webster 2019). The Joint Pledge is, at the time of writing, open for comments from AIIA members and the general public until the end of June 2019 (Webster 2019). While the wording is fairly generic when compared to other ethics and governance statements Webster (2019) points to the language of 'secure/safe and controllable' and 'self-discipline' as 'mesh[ing] with broader trends in Chinese digital governance'.

Finally, an expert group formed of researchers at Chinese universities and established by the Chinese Government Ministry of Science and Technology released its eight Governance Principles for the New Generation Artificial Intelligence: Developing

Responsible Artificial Intelligence in June 2019 (China Daily 2019). It has been reported that other experts, notably Kai-Fu Lee, made written submissions to the committee at earlier stages in their work (Laskai & Webster 2019). Again international cooperation is emphasized in the principles, including along with 'full respect' for AI development in other countries. A possibly novel inclusion is the idea of 'agile governance', that problems arising from AI can be addressed and resolved 'in a timely manner'. This principle reflects the rapidity of AI development and the difficulty in governing it through conventional procedures, for example through legislation which can take a long time to pass in China by which time the AI technology may have already changed. While 'agile policy-making' is a term also used by the EU High-Level Expert Panel, it is used in relation to e.g. the regulatory sandbox approach, as opposed to resolving problems, and is also not included in the Panel's Guidelines as a principle.

While, as mentioned above, Chinese tech corporations have been involved in AI ethics and governance initiatives both domestically in China and internationally in the form of the Partnership on AI, they also appear to be internally considering ethics in their AI activities. Tencent has its AI for Social Good programme and ARCC (Available, Reliance, Comprehensible, and Controllable) Principles (Si 2018) but does not appear at the time of writing to have an internal ethics board to review AI developments.

However, the principles set by these initiatives so far lack legal enforcement/enforceability and policy implications - like the AI ethics/governance guidelines elsewhere.

AI in Hong Kong

Under the 'One Country, Two Systems' framework, Hong Kong SAR remains a semi-autonomous region of China, with its own legal system until 2047. Its development, uptake and governance of AI present a different picture to that of mainland China. In a regional report for the IEEE written in 2017, Yu pointed to AI adoption and development in Hong Kong being somewhat fragmented and only a little behind regional neighbors but viewed

Hong Kong as having more progress to make 'before it can credibly tackle some of the legal, policy or ethical issues surrounding AI'.

Since that report was written, there has been one major development in Hong Kong. The Privacy Commissioner for Personal Data (PCPD), Hong Kong, issued an Ethical Accountability Framework in 2018, following industry consultation (but it is not clear if there was any consultation with academia and civil society). The discussion in the Framework explicitly links the issue of data ethics to AI, and acknowledges the additional guidance an ethical approach can give to the principles-based and technology-neutral legislation (the Privacy (Data Protection) Ordinance). The Framework includes a series of 'Enhanced Elements' and three 'recommended' Hong Kong Data Stewardship Values of 'Respectful, Beneficial and Fair' which were developed with the industry consultees, along with two assessment models for use by stakeholders. The Hong Kong Monetary Authority (2019) has encouraged 'authorised institutions' to adopt the Framework regarding personal data in the context of fintech development.

5. United States of America

Widely believed to rival only China in its domestic research and development of AI, the US has been less active institutionally regarding questions of ethics, governance and regulation compared to developments in China and the EU, until the recent Trump Administration Executive Order on Maintaining American Leadership in Artificial Intelligence from February 2019.

This Order has legal force, and creates an American AI Initiative guided by five high level principles and to be implemented by the National Science and Technology Council (NSTC) Select Committee on Artificial Intelligence. These principles include the US driving development of 'appropriate technical standards' and protecting 'civil liberties, privacy and American values' in AI applications 'to fully realize the potential for AI technologies for the American people'. Internationalization is included with the view of opening foreign markets for US AI technology and protecting the US's critical AI technology 'from acquisition by strategic competitors and adversarial nations'.

Furthermore, executive departments and agencies that engage in AI related activities such as developing it, providing educational grants and 'regulat[ing] and provid[ing] guidance for applications of AI technologies' must adhere to six strategic objectives including protection of 'American technology, economic and national security, civil liberties, privacy, and values' and ensuring that technical standards for AI 'minimize vulnerability to attacks from malicious actors and reflect Federal priorities for innovation, public trust, and public confidence in systems that use AI technologies; and develop international standards to promote and protect those priorities'.

The Order also contains some Guidance on Regulation of AI Applications, whereby agencies are to receive a memorandum from the Office of Management and Budget within 180 days to inform their regulatory and non-regulatory approaches to AI which 'advance American innovation while upholding civil liberties, privacy, and American values' and shall 'consider ways to reduce barriers to the use of AI technologies in order to promote their innovative application while protecting civil liberties, privacy, American values, and United States economic and national security'. A draft of this memorandum is to be made publicly available before it is sent to these agencies, which appears not to have happened at the time of writing. Finally, the National Institute of Standards and Technology (NIST) were tasked by the Executive Order with creating a plan for federal engagement in developing technical standards for reliable, robust, and trustworthy AI systems. In May 2019 NIST issued a Request for Information to this effect.

In addition, the US Department of Defence launched its AI Strategy, also in February 2019. The Strategy explicitly mentions US military rivals China and Russia investing in military AI 'including in applications that raise questions regarding international norms and human rights', as well as the perceived 'threat' of these developments to the US and 'the free and open international order'. As part of the Strategy, the Department asserts that it 'will articulate its vision and guiding principles for using AI in a lawful and ethical manner to promote our values', and will 'continue to share our aims, ethical guidelines, and safety procedures to encourage responsible AI development and use by other nations'.

The Department's Joint Artificial Intelligence Centre will, among other tasks, '[f]acilitate AI planning, policy, governance, ethics, safety, cyber security, and multilateral coordination'. As regards more detailed principles, the Department asserted that it would develop principles for AI ethics and safety in defence matters after multi-stakeholder consultations, with the promotion of the Department's views to a more global audience, with the seemingly intended consequence that its vision will inform a global set of military AI ethics.

As well as these recent interventions from the federal government, the US has a stronger record of AI ethics and governance activity from the private and not-for-profit sectors. Various US-headquartered/originating multinational tech corporations have issued ethics statements on their AI activities, notably the Microsoft AI Principles. Deep Mind (part of Google's Alphabet group of companies) also has its own Ethics and Society Principles. In 2019, Google itself announced that it had set up an AI Ethics committee of experts to inform its AI activities, but not long after this announcement, Google disbanded the committee, seemingly due to the controversial views of one panel member and the negative public reaction and reaction from Google employees (Turner 2019).

There are various not-for-profit organizations and foundations based in the US which have also been active in AI governance and ethics discussions. The Future of Life Institute released its 23 Asilomar AI Principles, developed in conjunction with their Beneficial AI conference in 2017. Participants in the process appeared to come mainly from academia and industry. Open AI, a mixed organization with for profit and not-for-profit wings, released its Open AI Charter, detailing the principles the organization uses to guide its activities in accordance with its mission that artificial general intelligence (systems which outperform humans at economically valuable work) benefits all humanity.

As regards applications of AI in the form of facial recognition technology, in May 2019 the city of San Francisco prohibited the use of facial recognition technology by city agencies and the police department - although the technology was seemingly not being used by the police department there prior to the ban (Sandler 2019). The prohibition was motivated by concerns about the inaccuracies in using facial recognition technology especially for people of colour, and about racial discrimination in how facial recognition technology has been deployed elsewhere to target specific, particularly racial, groups and communities (Sandler 2019).

6. Australia

Australia is in a unique situation as the only Western democracy without comprehensive enforceable protection of human rights (that is, no bill of rights, no comprehensive constitutional protection of rights). Despite this, there has been increasing attention in Australia on the human rights impacts of technology, and the development of an ethics framework for AI. Specifically, the Australian Human Rights Commission has commenced a Technology and Human Rights project, including releasing a white paper for public consultation, although a final report is yet to be published. Further, the Australian Government Department of Industry, Innovation and Science have recently released a discussion paper to inform the development of Australia's ethics framework for Artificial Intelligence (initial submissions on the discussion paper closed at the end of May 2019). In addition, in 2018, the Office of the Victorian Information Commissioner released an issues paper on Artificial Intelligence and Privacy.

The most prominent of these developments is the proposed Australian Ethical Framework currently under development by Data 61 and CSIRO in the Commonwealth Department of Industry, Innovation and Science. The discussion paper commences with an examination of existing ethical frameworks, principles and guidelines. The report includes a selection of case studies, these are largely international or US based, which overshadows the unique Australian (e.g. socio-political) context.

The report dedicates a chapter to considerations of 'data governance' (i.e. privacy and data protection) which has been critiqued extensively by a coalition of Australian privacy experts, as representing a fundamental misunderstanding of Australian privacy law (Salinger 2019). Further, there is a focus on matters of 'consent' where it may not be relevant in either current or future data processing landscapes. In addition, when discussing issues of data governance there is a need to distinguish between personal information and sensitive information, and also to consider sensitive inferences (see Wachter and Mittelstadt's work (2018) on a right to reasonable inferences).

The report sets forth a very narrow understanding of the negative impacts of AI for privacy, for example, a focus on data breaches or the potential for re-identification of de-identified data. Rather, there is a need to consider other harms, for example, such as those that could arise from automated decision-making. The report does indeed dedicate a chapter on automated decisions but does not consider or refer to regulatory approaches to respond or regulate to automated decision making, processing or profiling (for example, Article-22 of the EU's GDPR).Further, there is a need to consider the complexities of processing/profiling large sets of data, abstraction from data, including sensitive inferences, as mentioned above. The report then considers examples of AI in practice, and then outlines a proposed ethical framework.

Principles for Australia's AI Ethical Framework

The development of the proposed Australian AI ethical framework was guided by a steering committee comprising industry, government, community organizations, and CSIRO/ Data 61 researchers. It should also be noted that CSIRO/Data61 is a Commonwealth entity that is developing AI technology for the Commonwealth government. The discussion paper sets out eight core or key principles to form an ethical framework for AI, namely: generates net-benefits; do no harm; regulatory and legal compliance; privacy protection; fairness; transparency and explainability; contestability; and explainability.

The proposed Australian AI ethical framework is accompanied by a 'toolkit' of strategies, which appear to be attempts to operationalise the high level ethical principles in practice. The 'toolkit' indicates how the high-level ethical principles are intended to translate into practice. These include: impact assessments; internal/external review; risk assessments; best practice guidelines; industry standards; collaboration; mechanisms for monitoring and improvement; recourse mechanisms, and; consultation. Australia's ethical framework and the associated 'toolkit' are presently under development, and will continue to evolve and be refined on the basis of public submissions and consultation over the near future. In general, the proposed Australian principles do not seem very different to other ethical principles especially from other Western jurisdictions.

7. Reflections, issues and next steps

Here we offer some tentative reflections on the country/region profiles outlined above, and also the issue of the global governance of AI more generally which we set out here. Some of these reflections lead to further questions for further analysis of the different ethics and governance initiatives (and lack thereof in some cases).

(a) Have and have-nots

Of the large jurisdictions we have considered, it is interesting to note that the European Union and China seem most advanced in their consideration of ethical aspects of AI. The US may soon make up for lost time subsequent to the directions in the Executive Order from earlier this year. However, India stands alone as the one of the four 'large jurisdictions' under consideration which has not yet developed ethics guidelines for AI.

(b) Competition vs. collaboration

Themes of competition loom large over national/regional AI

policies, as regards competition with other 'large' countries or jurisdictions. It is widely believed and asserted that the US and China are the global forerunners in AI research and development and are in direct competition with each other (Cave and Óh Éigeartaigh 2018). This may be reflected in the US Executive Order being framed around preserving the US's competitive position, and also the Chinese ambition for China to become the global AI leader in 2030. This competition takes both economic and also security (including military) dimensions, especially in the latter case for state-used AI and AI technologies applied in public infrastructure.

However, there are also calls for global collaboration on AI ethics and governance, notably from the Chinese initiatives. This can be contrasted, on the face of it at least, with language from the US government initiatives which seems to reflect the 'America First' approach of the Trump Administration more broadly, whereby ethics and governance may be devised in the US for AI and then 'shared' or exported to the rest of the world. While less explicit, the European approaches which reference European legal texts such as the Charter of Fundamental Rights of the EU may foresee an attempt to export 'European values' regarding ethical AI globally, as de facto may be happening for data protection via the EU GDPR's extraterritorial reach.

Not only among the big powers, but also internally do we also see some economic competition, particularly in the case of the EU where there are EU-level AI initiatives and strategies, but also possibly competing initiatives at the national level in some Member States. The relationship between Member States and the EU centrally may influence the development of such national strategies, especially when that relationship has broken down, as in the case of the UK leaving the EU. The UK's own national AI strategies and attempt to position the UK as a leader in ethical AI ought to be considered against this backdrop, especially when its European competitor Germany is also positioning itself in this space.

For smaller countries which may not be able to compete with the 'big boys' of global AI, Austria suggests that they may be willing to engage in less ethical projects to attract attention and investment (although this may also be the case for India if it positions itself as an AI 'garage'), and the Australian example shows how they may be 'followers' rather than 'leaders' inasmuch as they receive ethical principles and approaches formulated by other, similar but larger countries.

(c) Similarities and differences

In many of the AI ethics/governance statements, we see similar if not the same concept reappear, such as transparency explainability, accountability etc. Hagendorff (2019) has pointed out that these principles, frequently encountered, are often 'the most easily operationalized mathematically' which may account partly for their presence in many initiatives.

 Some form of 'privacy' or 'data protection' also features frequently, even in the absence of robust privacy/data protection laws as in the US example. In the case of India, a lack of data protection law at the time of writing is viewed as a reason explaining why there is no AI ethics/governance document yet issued there.

As mentioned earlier, some AI ethics initiatives present some differences, both in terms of which actors have formulated them (public vs. private sector; civil society involvement; academic expertise etc), the content of principles articulated (e.g. China's 'agile governance') and the general framing of the statements of principles.

Nevertheless, behind some of these shared principles may lay different cultural, legal and philosophical understandings. This is a point to interrogate further in future work.

(d) What's not included?

Another important issue is what is not included in AI ethics/ governance initiatives, i.e. what is missing from the lists of principles. Is reference made to other government or corporate initiatives which may contradict the principles? To what extent are the 'hidden costs' of AI made visible and internalised, such as the energy and other human resources and raw materials needed for the systems (Hagendorff 2019)? The language of sustainability in the EU High-Level Expert Panel's Recommendations does acknowledge the environmental and sustainability aspects and concerns regarding the creation and use of AI technologies. A further question is the extent to which the very use of AI in the first place is ethically interrogated by AI and ethics and governance statements, or just assumed to be used, or will inevitably be used. And what about the broader social contexts in which AI finds itself deployed - this seems rarely if ever to be considered in AI ethics/ governance initiatives explicitly.

(e) What's already there?

There are already different areas of existing law, policy and governance which will apply to AI and its implementations including technology and industrial policy, data protection, intellectual property, fundamental rights, private law, administrative law, etc. Sometimes these existing regimes are taken account of in AI ethics/ governance initiatives but in many cases, they are not, or indeed in the Australian example, may have been mischaracterized and misunderstood.

 While less 'exciting' and 'novel' than proposing new governance frameworks, important work needs to be done to understand better the interactions of these existing frameworks with AI and the extent to which further action is necessary, or could be guided, as has been called for in the EU. It is important for those to whom AI ethics and governance guidelines area addressed to be aware that they may need to consider, and comply with, further principles and norms in their AI research, development and application beyond those articulated in AI-specific guidelines.

(f) Implementation and enforceability

Almost all of the AI ethics and governance documents we have considered do not have the force of binding law. The US Executive Order is an exception in that regard, although constitutes more a series of directions to government agencies rather than a detailed set of legally binding ethical principles. This situation overall leads to concerns about 'ethics washing' (Wagner 2018; Watts 2019) as mentioned earlier in relation to the EU High-Level Expert Panel activities, but on a broader scale: that ethics and governance initiatives without the binding force of law are mere 'window dressing' while unethical uses of AI by governments and corporations continue. Indeed, in various of the countries and regions we have examined, despite the existence of ethical guidelines on AI, unethical AI applications exist, which may fail a test against those very principles.

This also leads to a broader question about the operationalization of ethical and governance initiatives, especially those which articulate principles and norms for AI. Can they and will they actually are implemented into law, business and technical practices in public and private sector AI in their respective countries, regions and corporations? How will this be assessed? Will there be meaningful consequences if this does not happen?

Some ethics statements also include regulatory or legal compliance as an ethical principle, such as in the Australian example. While this may acknowledge that existing laws and regulations may not have been complied with in the past by AI researchers, developers and implementers, such an ethical principle may seem odd, inasmuch as it may be considered the law ought to be complied with anyway. However, such an ethical principle also does not account for situations where the existing law may be unethical or otherwise lacking. A further issue arises around organizations or researchers from a particular country or region which does have AI ethics/governance principles 'jurisdiction shopping' to a location which does not nor has laxer standards to research and develop AI with less 'constraints'? This off shoring of AI development to 'less ethical' countries may already be happening and is something that should in particular be addressed in national/regional ethics and governance initiatives.

A historical perspective is also warranted regarding the likelihood of success for AI ethics/governance initiatives, in the form of examining the success or otherwise of previous attempts to govern new technologies, such as biotech and the Internet, or to insert ethics in other domains such as medicine (see Mittelstadt 2019). While there are specificities for each new technology, different predecessor technologies from which it has sprung, as well as different social, economic and political conditions, looking to the historical trajectory of new technologies and their governance may teach us some lessons for AI governance and ethics.

(g). Who is involved?

A key question for analyzing AI ethics and governance activities further in future work is examining which actors are involved in their processes of formulation - at the global or national levels. To what extent is academic experts and civil society groups involved and to what extent are their voices and input heard and considered? Do civil society groups which are involved represent the public in practice, or subsections of the public? Who funds the groups and initiatives? Is there enough genuine public consultation to ensure AI has a social license to operate in a particular country, or for particular applications? Is the formulation of AI ethics and governance largely a technocratic exercise? To what extent are participants in AI and its governance and ethics debates and initiatives demographically representative of the population at large? Hagendorff (2019) has criticized a lack of gender diversity in the AI field as an example of how ethical goals are being 'underachieved'.

We have identified scope for further work on AI ethics and global governance in the preceding paragraphs as well as earlier in this report when we outlined the limitations of this work. Further work may also be conducted to continue to track and analyze emerging and new AI ethics and governance initiatives, as well as appraise how existing initiatives are being implemented. We as collective and as individual researchers may do some of this work ourselves, but we also look to such further work being done by others. To that extent, if you are interested in collaborating with some or all of us, please get in touch!

Artificial Intelligence Governance and Ethics: Global Perspectives: Angela Daly, Thilo Hagendorff, Li Hui, Monique Mann, Vidushi

Marda, Ben Wagner, Wei Wang and Saskia Witteborn. This report is supported by Angela Daly's Chinese University of Hong Kong 2018-2019 Direct Grant for Research 2018-2019 'Governing the Future: How are Major Jurisdictions Tackling the Issue of Artificial Intelligence, Law and Ethics?' Released under a Creative Commons CC BY-ND Attribution-No Derives licence.

Authors

Angela Daly, PhD, is a socio-legal scholar working on transnational regulation of new (digital) technologies. She is the author of Socio-Legal Aspects of the 3D Printing Revolution (Palgrave 2016) and Private Power, Online Information Flows and EU Law: Mind the Gap (Hart 2016) and co-editor of Good Data (Institute of Network Cultures 2019). She holds a PhD in Law from the European University Institute. Thilo Hagendorff, PhD, is a media and technology ethicist. He received his doctorate in 2013 with a sociological thesis. He has been a research associate at the International Centre for Ethics in the Sciences and Humanities (IZEW) at the University of Tuebingen (Germany) since 2013. Li Hui, PhD, is an associate research fellow at the Shanghai Institute for Science of Science (China). He received his doctorate majoring in history of science in 2011 from Shanghai Jiao Tong University. Monique Mann, PhD, is the Vice Chancellor's Research Fellow in Technology and Regulation at the Faculty of Law Queensland University of Technology (Australia). She is an Adjunct Researcher with the Law, Science, Technology and Society (LSTS) Research Centre at Vrije Universiteit Brussel (Belgium). Ben Wagner, PhD, is an Assistant Professor and Director of the Privacy & Sustainable Computing Lab at Vienna University of Economics and Business (Austria). Saskia Witteborn, PhD, is Associate Professor in the School of Journalism and Communication at the Chinese University of Hong Kong. Wei Wang is a PhD candidate at the University of Hong Kong Faculty of Law.

Notes and References

Introduction

1   Fixing the EU intelligence Crisis, Musa Khan Jalalzai, introduction pages 2,3,4

2   Regulating surveillance, respecting private life, Open Rights Group (ORG). Digital Surveillance, Why the Snoopers' Charter is the wrong approach: A call for targeted and accountable investigatory powers. Barrister Angela Patrick, (Director of Human Rights Policy at JUSTICE.

3   Regulating surveillance, respecting private life. Open Rights Group (ORG). Digital Surveillance. Why the Snoopers' Charter is the wrong approach: A call for targeted and accountable investigatory powers. Dr. Richard Clayton.

4   The TruePublica report, 23 May 2019

5   Ibid

6   the Guardian report, 13 August 2019

7   Big Brother Watch Report, 10 July 2019

8   Surveillance by intelligence services: fundamental rights safeguards and remedies in the EU Volume II: field perspectives and legal update, October 2017, This report is FRA's second publication addressing a European Parliament request for in-depth research on the impact of surveillance on fundamental rights. The European Union Agency for Fundamental Rights (FRA) is the EU's centre of fundamental rights expertise.

9   Intelligence in Vex, Musa Khan Jalalzai, Vij publishing New Delhi, 2019

10   Ibid

11   Ibid

12   The Guardian 12 July 2019

13 Intelligence in Vex, Musa Khan Jalalzai, Vij publishing New Delhi, 2019

14 Fixing the EU intelligence Crisis, Musa Khan Jalalzai, Algora New York 2017

15 Dr. Gustav Gressel paper, 25 June, 2019

16 Countering Violent Extremism and Radicalization that Lead to Terrorism: Ideas, Recommendations, and Good Practices from the OSCE Region. Report by Professor Peter R. Neumann OSCE Chairperson in Office's Special Representative on Countering Radicalization and Violent Extremism International Centre for the Study of Radicalization (ICSR), King's College London, 28 September 2017.

17 Fixing the EU intelligence Crisis, Musa Khan Jalalzai, Algora New York 2017

18 ibid

19 Ambient accountability: intelligence services in Europe and the decline of state secrecy, Richard J. Aldrich and Daniela Richterova, Politics and International Studies, University of Warwick, Coventry, United Kingdom, West European Politics, 2018 https://doi.org/10.1080/01402382.2017.1415780, https://warwick.ac.uk/fac/soc/pais/people/aldrich/secrets/final.wep.proofs.pdf

20 The Guardian, 02 May 2019

21 Telegraph 04 May 2019-09-08

22 National Security Council leaks 'undermine officials' confidence to speak truth to power', Civil Service World, Richard Johnstone, 25 April 2019, https://www.civilserviceworld.com/articles/news/national-security-council-leaks-%E2%80%98undermine-officials%E2%80%99-confidence-speak-truth-power%E2%80%99

23 Fixing the EU intelligence Crisis, Musa Khan Jalalzai, Algora New York 2017

24 Ibid

25 Surveillance by intelligence services: fundamental rights safeguards and remedies in the EU Volume II: field perspectives and legal update, October 2017, This report is FRA's second publication addressing a European Parliament request for in-depth research on the impact of surveillance on fundamental rights. The European Union Agency for Fundamental Rights (FRA) is the EU's centre of fundamental rights expertise.

26 Intelligence in Vex, Musa Khan Jalalzai, Vij publishing New Delhi, 2019

27 Intelligence and Accountability Principles: Dilemma for Legitimacy in Spain and Brazil, Yauri Miranda, Jaseff Raziel, University of the Basque Country (UPV/EHU, Taken from the website of Research Institute for European and American Studies (www.rieas.gr), 9 June 2019

Chapter 1: Tight-Corner of Intelligence and Surveillance Mechanism within the European Union

1 Intelligence in Vex. Intelligence in Vex: The UK and EU Intelligence Agencies Operate in a State of Fret. Musa Khan Jalalzai, Vij Books India Pvt Ltd, 30 Nov. 2018

2 How the Islamic State Rose, Fell and Could Rise Again in the Maghreb. International Crisis Group Report-178, Middle East and North Africa, 24 July 2017.

3 Fixing the EU Intelligence Crisis: Intelligence Sharing, Law Enforcement and the Threat of Chemical, Biological and Nuclear Terrorism. Musa Khan Jalalzai, Algora Publishing, 15 Aug 2016

4 Ibid

5 European Union Intelligence Analysis Centre (INTCEN): Next Stop to an Agency? By: John M. Nomikos, Journal of Mediterranean and Balkan intelligence.

6 Intelligence in Vex. Intelligence in Vex: The UK and EU Intelligence Agencies Operate in a State of Fret. Musa Khan Jalalzai. Vij Books India Pvt. Ltd, 30 Nov. 2018.

7 British National Security Capability Review Including the Second Annual Report on Implementation of the National Security Strategy and Strategic Defense and Security Review, 2015-2018.

8 The Guardian, 04 June 2018

9 Independent, 01 September 2017

10 Ibid, 23 March 2018

11 National Security Capability Review, 2017

12 Keeping Europe Safe: Counterterrorism for the Continent, David Omand, Foreign Affairs, September/October 2016

13 The Guardian, 03 June 2018

14 Ibid, 03 June 2018

15 The UK's Changing Democracy: The 2018 Democratic Audit Report. Edited by Patrick Dunleavy, Alice Park and Ros Taylor, http://www.democraticaudit.com/the-uks-changingdemocracy-the-2018-democratic-audit/.

16 The Guardian, 21 January 2015

17 06 November 2013, the BBC Report

18 Germany's Intelligence Services Reform Stocks controversy, Christoph Zeiher, translated by: Sam Morgan, The EUROACTIVE Germany, 21 October 2016, https://www.euractiv.com/section/justice-home-affairs/news/germanys-intelligence-servicereform-stokes-controversy/

19 Spy Chiefs call for continues EU Intelligence-Sharing after Brexit, The Belfast Telegraph, 16 February, 2018

20 The Guardian, 14 May 2018

21 Ibid, 20 June 2018

22 Daily Times, 07 February 2017

23 Intelligence and decision making within the Common Foreign and Security Policy-2015, Fagersten Bjorn. SIEPS. And his second paper is cited as, Bureaucratic Resistance to International Intelligence cooperation-The Case of Europol, 2010. http://www.sieps.se/en/publications/2015/intelligence-and-decision-making-within-the-common-foreign-and-security-policy-201522epa/

24 The Guardian Newspaper, 17 January 2018 Intelligence and Accountability Principles: Dilemma for Legitimacy in Spain and Brazil. Yauri Miranda and Jaseff Raziel

Chapter 2: Britain's Changing Security Perceptions: the Country's National Security Challenges are Amplifying by the Day

1 Intelligence in Vex: The EU and UK intelligence agencies are in a state of fret. Musa Khan Jalalzai. Vij Publishing, India, 2018

2 Ibid

3 The Independent Police Complaints Commission, https://www.gov.uk/government/organisations/independent-police-complaint-commission

4   Ibid

5   Ibid

6   The UK's Changing Democracy: The 2018 Democratic Audit, edited by: Patrick Dunleavy, Alice Park, and Ros Taylor. LSE Press, 2018

7   On 28 June 2018, the UK Parliamentary Intelligence and Security Committee released the torture and rendition report.

8   Daily Mail, 03 June 2018, https://www.dailymail.co.uk/news/article-5800457/British-spies-accused-sharing-intelligence-obtained-torture.html

9   The Independent, 28 June 2018, https://www.independent.co.uk/news/uk/home-news/uk-torture-rendition-detainees-treatment-isc-mi5-mi6-911-war-terror-a8421856.html

10   Intelligence in Vex: The EU and UK intelligence agencies are in a state of fret. Musa Khan Jalalzai. Vij Publishing, India, 2018

11   Ibid

12   Interception of communication Code of Practice Pursuant to section 71 of the ROPA Act 2000, Interception of Communications Code of Practice Pursuant to section 71 of the Regulation of Investigatory Powers Act 2000 February 2015

13   Ibid

14   Intelligence in Vex: The EU and UK intelligence agencies are in a state of fret. Musa Khan Jalalzai. Vij Publishing, India, 2018

15   Ibid

16   Ibid

17   Reforming Surveillance in the UK, The Don't Spy on US campaign of various organizations that defend privacy report, September 2014, https://www.dontspyonus.org.uk/assets/files/pdfs/reports/DSOU_Reforming_surveillance.pdf

18   Ibid

19   Ibid; NSA Report: Liberty and Security in a Changing World, The President's Review Group on Intelligence and Communications Technologies, Richard A. Clarke, Michael J. Morell, Geoffrey R. Stone, Cass R. Sunstein, Peter Swire, Princeton University Press, 31 Mar 2014

20   Intelligence in Vex: The EU and UK intelligence agencies are in a state of fret. Musa Khan Jalalzai. Vij Publishing, India, 2018

21   Ibid

22   Press release of Privacy International: UK intelligence agencies admits unlawfully spying on Privacy International, 25 September 2018, https://privacyinternational.org/press-release/2283/press-release-uk-intelligence-agency-admits-unlawfully-spying-privacy

23   Ibid

24   Ibid

25   Ibid

26   Fact Sheet: Investigatory Power, HO News Team 17 June 2019, https://homeofficemedia.blog.gov.uk/2019/06/17/fact-sheet-what-are-investigatory-powers/. Securing the Insecure States in Britain and Europe. Musa Khan Jalalzai, Algora new York, 2017

27   Ibid

28   On February 16, 2015, The Guardian reported that a man from Liverpool had been charged with attempting to obtain a chemical weapon.

29   Daily Times, 12 September 2014

30   Ibid, Policy Paper, 04 December 2013

31   Amnesty International, 03 July 2015

32   BBC, 06 February, 2015

33   The inquiry was prompted by the revelations from documents leaked by former CIA contractor Edward Snowden, The Guardian, 12 March 2015

34   Ibid

Chapter 3: Law Enforcement, Security Sector Reform and the Fight against Radicalization, Drug Trafficking and Terrorism in UK

1   Law Enforcement in the United States, James A. Conser, Rebecca Paynich, Terry Gingerich, Terry E. Gingerich, Jones & Bartlett Publishers, 21 Oct 2011

2   Daily Times, 07 April 2015

3   Ibid

4   07 July 2017, TR News reported London witnessed up to three acid attacks every week

5   National Crime Agency Annual Reports, 2016-17

6   The Guardian, 29 March 2016

7   BBC 11 March 2015

8   Ibid

9   Ibid

10   March 9, 2015, BBC reported the police approach to law enforcement as peculiar, which typically involved waiting until a crime committed and then attempted to tackle it and arrest the criminal.

11   The Independent, 23 January 2015, and BBC 11 March 2015 November 2014

12   On November 6, 2014, The Guardian reported that Sir Bernard Hogan-Howe, commissioner of the Metropolitan police in London, told a conference of senior US police chiefs that law enforcement agencies in the UK had lost the public's trust after the disclosures on government surveillance made by Mr. Edward Snowden.

13   Daily Times, 18 November 2014

14   On 06 November, 2014, The Guardian reported Sir Bernard Hogan-Howe, commissioner of the Metropolitan police in London, told a conference of senior police chiefs that law enforcement agencies in the UK lost the public's trust after the disclosures on government surveillance made by Mr. Edward Snowden.

15   Daily Mail, 25 November 2014, and details of National Crime Agency website

16   Ibid

17   Daily Times, 02 December 2014

18   Telegraph, 22 January 2017

19   The Guardian 24 August 2016

20   On 22 January 2017, Guardian reported a police officer was shot by terrorists in Northern Ireland

21   BBC, 25 August 2016

22   BBC, 25 August 2016

23   International Business Times, 05 August 2016

24   Police Pay: Winsor Review Updated in 2015. Tom Winsor conducted an independent review of police officers and staff remuneration and

condition, Part-1 Report, March 2011. https://www.gov.uk/government/uploads/system/uploads/attachment_data/file/229006/8024.pdf

25   Carnegie Europe, 18 February 2015, and the Independent February 2015

26   On 07 August 2019, the Guardian reported Britain's most senior counterterrorism expert Neil Basu statement about the police and security service inability to tackle violent extremism.

27   On 09 August 2019, the Guardian reported sale of weapons on the Internet in Britain 15 National Cyber Crime Unit, http://www.nationalcrimeagency.gov.uk/about-us/what-we-do/national-cyber-crime-unit, Daily Times, 18

28   Telegraph, 16 November 2012

29   Daily Times, 24 January 2017

30   Ibid

31   Sputnik News 19 January 2017

32   Ibid

33   Towards greater public confidence: A proposal review of the current police complaints system for England and Wales, Deborah Glass, March 2016

34   Ibid

Chapter 4: Bulk Surveillance in the Digital Age: Rethinking the Human Rights Law Approach to the Bulk Monitoring of Communication DATA. Daragh Murray and Pete Fussey

1   Also referred to as 'metadata': for further discussion see Section 2 below.

2   See, eg, the Investigatory Powers Act 2016 (UK), Parts 4, 6 and 7.

3   Government of the United Kingdom, 'Operational Case for Bulk Powers', 2016, para 1.7.

4   In the digital age, individuals produce a significant quantity of communications data. This can be used to make revealing inferences about specific individuals, providing insights into, inter alia, their health, sexual orientation and political affiliations: see further below Sections 2 and 5.1.

5   See, in this regard, ECtHR, Szabo and Vissy v Hungary, App no 37138/14, 12 January 2016, para 57; Council of Europe Commissioner for Human Rights, 'Democratic and Effective Oversight of National Security Services', May 2015, 19–27.

6   See, in this regard, Asaf Lubin, '"We Only Spy on Foreigners": The Myth of a Universal Right to Privacy and the Practice of Foreign Mass Surveillance' (2018) 18 Chicago Journal of International Law 502; Ashley Deeks, 'An International Legal Framework for Surveillance' (2015) 55 Virginia Journal of International Law 291.

7   This article does not intend to analyze the Investigatory Powers Act or its compliance with the requirements of human rights law. Rather, it is presented as an example of modern domestic legislation that regulates advanced surveillance practices. For further information on the Act itself, see Simon McKay, Blackstone's Guide to the Investigatory Powers Act 2016 (Oxford University Press 2017).

8   Other European surveillance regimes are discussed in European Union Fundamental Rights Agency, 'Surveillance by Intelligence Services: Fundamental Rights, Safeguards and Remedies in the EU', Vol I: Member States' Legal Frameworks (2017).

9   See ECtHR, S and Marper v United Kingdom, App nos 30562/04 and 30566/04, 4 December 2008, para 101.

10   This is broadly similar to the test established in relation to the International Convention on Civil and Political Rights (ICCPR) ((entered into force 23 March 1976) 999 UNTS 171) and the American Convention on Human Rights (Pact of San José, Costa Rica (entered into force 18 July 1978) 1144 UNTS 123). In these treaties reference is made to necessity and proportionality, but not always to the test of necessity 'in a democratic society'. See, for instance, the discussion of necessity in UN Human Rights Committee, General Comment No 34, Article 19: Freedoms of Opinion and Expression (12 September 2011), UN Doc CCPR/C/GC/34.

11   See, eg, ECtHR, Weber and Saravia v Germany, App no 54934/00, 29 June 2006, paras 103–104.

12   ie, how 'useful' bulk surveillance techniques are, in light of the legitimate aims pursued.

13   The UK High Court classified communications data into three broad categories: subscriber data, service data, and traffic data: see Davis and Others v Secretary of State for the Home Department [2015] EWHC 2092, [13].

14 For instance, normal use of a Smartphone will indicate the user's location history, the identity of everyone with whom he or she communicates (over email, phone or messaging), the time and duration of this communication, and the user's internet search history.

15 See, eg, Investigatory Powers Act (n 2) s 61; UN Human Rights Council

16 Report of the Special Rapporteur on the Promotion and Protection of the Right to Freedom of Opinion and Expression – Frank La Rue (17 April 2013), UN Doc A/HRC/23/40, para 15.

17 David Anderson, Independent Reviewer of Terrorism Legislation, 'A Question of Trust: Report of the Investigatory Powers Review', June 2015, 129.

18 For example, computational science research has consistently demonstrated how only a few partial scraps of data can be merged to reveal a comprehensive picture of someone's identity. This includes the sufficiency of only four spatiotemporal points to identify 95% of both an individual's identity and their unique travel patterns: see Yves-Alexandre de Montjoye and others, 'Unique in the Crowd: The Privacy Bounds of Human Mobility' (2013) 3 Nature Scientific Reports 1.

19 Joined Cases C-203/15 and C-698/15 Tele2 Sverige AB v Post-och telestyrelsen and Secretary of State for the Home Department v Watson and Others, Opinion of Advocate General Saugmandsgaard Øe, 19 July 2016, ECLI:EU:C:2016:572, [253] (Tele2 Sverige AB, AG Opinion).

20 Report of the Special Rapporteur (n 15) para 42.

21 This is partially because of the complexity associated with understanding and accurately analysing speech, and the difficulty in effectively automating this practice.

22 Tele2 Sverige AB, AG Opinion (n 19) [257]–[259].

23 See, generally, Viktor Mayer-Schönberger and Kenneth Cukier, Big Data: A Revolution that Will Transform How We Live, Work, and Think (John Murray 2013).

24 ie, the collection of communications data relating to a specific individual, initiated on the basis of a reasonable suspicion that that individual is engaged in criminal activity.

25 See, inter alia, David Lyon, Surveillance after Snowden (Polity Press

2015).

26 Investigatory Powers Act (n 2) s 87. If this retained data is accessed by the intelligence and security services and therefore becomes 'operationally relevant', it is possible that it may be retained by these agencies for significant periods of time, and also potentially reassembled into new forms in the future, thus ensuring a more enduring legacy. This may be a loophole in existing legislation, such as the UK Investigatory Powers Act, which has the effect of facilitating the retention of communications data for significantly longer than envisaged in the legislation.

27 Investigatory Powers Act (n 2) s 61(7)(a), (b) and (f), respectively.

28 See ECtHR, Barbulescu v Romania, App no 61496/08, Judgment, 12 January 2016, para 36.

29 The ECtHR examined the right to private life and freedom of expression together in Telegraaf Media Nederland Landelijke Media BV and Others v The Netherlands, App no 39315/06, 22 November 2012, para 88. The CJEU similarly discussed both privacy and expression in Joined Cases C-203/15 and C-698/15 Tele2 Sverige AB v Post-och telestyrelsen and Secretary of State for the Home Department v Watson and Others, Judgment, 21 December 2016, ECLI:EU:C:2016:970, [92], [93]. For further discussion on the content of the right to freedom of expression, see UN Human Rights Committee (n 10).

30 A similar test is applied when evaluating compliance with the ICCPR (n 10): UN Human Rights Committee (n 10) para 22.

31 See, eg, Operational Case for Bulk Powers (n 3); Anderson (n 17); David Anderson, Independent Reviewer of Terrorism Legislation, 'Report of the Bulk Powers Review', August 2016; Privacy and Civil Liberties Oversight Board, 'Report on the Telephone Records Program Conducted under Section 215 of the USA Patriot Act and on the Operations of the Foreign Intelligence Surveillance Court', 23 January 2014.

32 Anderson (2016), ibid para 4.12.

33 Operational Case for Bulk Powers (n 3) para 1.7.

34 Anderson (n 17) para 9.28.

35 Operational Case for Bulk Powers (n 3) para 5.6.

36 ibid 28.

37 ibid para 5.2.

38 ibid paras 5.2–5.3.

39 ibid para 3.13.

40 For instance, a specific individual, or a suspect's device.

41 Operational Case for Bulk Powers (n 3) para 3.17.

42 Anderson (n 17) 337.

43 See, eg, Carpenter v United States, 585 US _ (2018), 12.

44 In the US context, see Privacy and Civil Liberties Oversight Board (n 31) 146.

45 Operational Case for Bulk Powers (n 3) para 9.6.

46 ibid para 9.5.

47 National Research Council of the National Academies, Bulk Collection of Signals Intelligence: Technical Options (National Academy of Sciences 2015) 57.

48 ie, through smartphone location data.

49 National Research Council of the National Academies (n 47) 52.

50 This is particularly useful in the cyber defence context.

51 Operational Case for Bulk Powers (n 3) para 9.18.

52 For example, the UK police and Crown Prosecution Service are reported to have highlighted three benefits of retained data (Anderson (n 17) para 9.45):

(a) Conspirators become more guarded in their use of communications as the moment of a crime approaches. Older data may therefore be the best evidence against them. (a)It may be relatively easy to arrest the minor players in a drugs importation or smuggling ring. But by going through their historic communications data, it may become possible to trace the bigger players who have taken care to remain in the background.

(b) A time lapse between the incident and the identification of a suspect will mean that old data is needed.

53 For further examples highlighting the utility of retained data provided by the French government, see Tele2 Sverige AB, AG Opinion (n 19) [183].

54 Operational Case for Bulk Powers (n 3) paras 1.8 and 4.5.

55 ibid para 1.8.

56 ibid.

57 Government of the United Kingdom, 'Operational Case for the Use of Communications Data by Public Authorities' (undated) 5.

58 Anderson (n 17) para 9.22.

59 Szabo and Vissy v Hungary (n 5) para 73.

60 'Case Study: Protecting Northern Ireland' in Operational Case for Bulk Powers (n 3) 39.

61 ibid.

62 'Case Study: Preventing A Kidnap' in Operational Case for Bulk Powers (n 3) 40.

63 Anderson (n 17) para 9.45.

64 ibid.

65 Of course, evidence of a vital role may be present but restricted on national security grounds.

66 Anderson (n 31) para 4.12.

67 For wide ranging reviews of such impacts see Pete Fussey, 'Beyond Liberty, Beyond Security: The Politics of Public Surveillance' (2008) 3 British Politics 120; David Lyon, Surveillance Society: Monitoring Everyday Life (Open University Press 2001); John Gilliom and Torin Monahan, Super Vision: An Introduction to the Surveillance Society (University of Chicago Press 2013).

68 This may include, for instance, accessing particular information, communicating with particular individuals or organizations, and attending certain events.

69 See Human Rights Committee, Aduayom and Others v Togo, Communication Nos 422/1990, 423/1990 and 424/1990, UN Doc CCPR/C/51/D/422/1990, 423/1990, 424/1990 (30 June 1994), art 7.4; Abrams v United States, 250 US 616 (1919), dissenting opinion of Justice Oliver Wendell Holmes.

70 Gregory L White and Phillip G Zimbardo, 'The Chilling Effects of Surveillance: Deindividuation and Reactance', Stanford University Technical Report prepared for the Office of Naval Research, May 1975, http:// www.dtic.mil/get-tr-doc/pdf?AD=ADA013230.

71 ibid 14.

72 ibid 5.

73 See Martin Scheinin, 'Report of the Special Rapporteur on the Promotion and Protection of Human Rights and Fundamental Freedoms while Countering Terrorism (28 December 2009), UN Doc A/HRCD/13/37, para 33; Joined Cases C-293/12 and C-594/12 Digital Rights Ireland v Minister for Communications and Others, Judgment, 8 April 2014, ECLI:EU:C:2014:238, [28]; Tele2 Sverige AB, judgment (n 29) [92]. Also, although a chilling effect is not directly discussed, see Szabo and Vissy v Hungary (n 5) para 68.

74 See, generally, Glenn Greenwald, No Place to Hide: Edward Snowden, the NSA, and the U.S. Surveillance State (Hamish Hamilton 2014); Ian Brown 'Social Media Surveillance' in Robin Mansell and others (eds), The International Encyclopedia of Digital Communication and Society (Wiley 2015) 1.

75 Pew Research Center, 'Americans' Privacy Strategies Post-Snowden', 16 March 2015, http://www.pewinternet. org/2015/03/16/Americans-Privacy-Strategies-Post-Snowden.

76 PEN America, 'Chilling Effects: NSA Surveillance Drives U.S. Writers to Self-Censor', 12 November 2013, https://pen.org/sites/default/files/2014-08-01_Full%20Report_Chilling%20Effects%20w%20Color%20cover-UPDATED.pdf.77 ibid 6.

78 Elizabeth Stoycheff, 'Under Surveillance: Examining Facebook's Spiral of Silence Effects in the Wake of NSA Internet Monitoring' (2016) 93 Journalism and Mass Communication Quarterly 296.

79 See generally, inter alia, Dawinder S Sidhu, 'The Chilling Effect of Government Surveillance Programs on the Use of the Internet by Muslim-Americans' (2007) 7 University of Maryland Law Journal of Race, Religion, Gender and Class 375; Amory Starr and others, 'The Impacts of State Surveillance on Political Assembly and Association: A Socio-Legal Analysis' (2008) 31(3) Qualitative Sociology 251; William Bloss, 'Escalating US Police Surveillance after 9/11: An Examination of Causes and Effects' (2007) 4(3) Surveillance and Society 208.

80 Clapper v Amnesty International USA, 568 US 398 (2013) III (B). This case focused on s 702 of FISA. A 2008 amendment allowed the Attorney General and the Director of National Intelligence (Clapper, in this instance) to collect intelligence on individuals reasonably believed to be outside the US. Several US-located civil society groups argued that because they may be in contact with individuals subject

to these surveillance measures, they might themselves become objects of scrutiny, with their communications and other interactions monitored.

Among other arguments, the plaintiffs argued that such surveillance activities exerted a chilling effect on their First Amendment rights.

81 Jon Penney, 'Chilling Effects: Online Surveillance and Wikipedia Use' (2016) 31 Berkeley Technology Law Journal 117. This study offers empirical evidence of chilling effects on online searches relating to Wikipedia arti- cles following Edward Snowden's revelations of June 2013 and the publicity that followed. The study identifies a reduction of 995,085 (over 30%) visits to Wikipedia sites that could be deemed subject to government surveillance (such as those discussing terrorism, suicide attack and Al-Qaeda, among others).

82 ibid 147.

83 inter alia, Clapper v Amnesty International USA (n 80) III(B).

84 Samuel Nunn, 'Seeking Tools for the War on Terror: A Critical Assessment of Emerging Technologies in Law Enforcement' (2003) 26 Policing: An International Journal of Police Strategies and Management 454.

85 ibid.

86 Pete Fussey, 'Protecting Britain's Crowded Spaces from Terrorist Attacks: Key Criminological Reflections' in Andrew Silke (ed), Psychology, Terrorism and Counter-Terrorism (Routledge 2010) 164.

87 Tyler Wall and Torin Monahan, 'Surveillance and Violence from Afar: The Politics of Drones and Liminal Security-scapes' (2011) 15 Theoretical Criminology 239.

88 TEMPORA was a secret GCHQ initiative that infiltrated over 200 fibre optic cables carrying internet traffic. This allowed detailed access to both the content and metadata of enormous quantities of global internet information.

89 See, further, Robert K Merton, 'Social Structure and Anomie' (1938) 3 American Sociological Review 672; Edwin M Lemert, Social Pathology: A Systematic Approach to the Theory of Sociopathic Behavior (McGraw-Hill 1951).

90 See, further, Howard S Becker, Outsiders: Studies in the Sociology of Deviance (Free Press 1963).

91 See, further, Clive Norris and Gary Armstrong, The Maximum Sur-

veillance Society (Berg 1999).

92   Abigail A Sewell and Kevin A Jefferson, 'Collateral Damage: The Health Effects of Invasive Police Encounters in New York City' (2016) 93 Journal of Urban Health: Bulletin of the New York Academy of Medicine 42.

93   Abigail A Sewell, Kevin A Jefferson and Hedwig Lee, 'Living under Surveillance: Gender, Psychological Distress, and Stop-Question-and-Frisk Policing in New York City' (2015) 156 Social Science & Medicine 1.

94   For authoritative critique on the eroding boundaries between the corrections estate and heavily policed urban spaces see, inter alia, Loic Wacquant, 'The New "Peculiar Institution": On the Prison as Surrogate Ghetto' (2000) 4 Theoretical Criminology 377.

95   Basia Spalek, 'Community Policing, Trust and Muslim Communities in relation to "New Terrorism"' (2010) 38 Politics and Policy 789.

96   Szabo and Vissy v Hungary (n 5) para 73.

97   ie, ensuring both the protection of the right to life, and the right to freedom of expression or the right to privacy. 98 Jonathan Mayer, Patrick Mutchler and John C Mitchell, 'Evaluating the Privacy Properties of Telephone Metadata', (2016) 113(20) PNAS 5536, 5540; doi 10.1073/pnas.1508081113.

99   Tele2 Sverige AB, AG Opinion (n 19) [257].

100   ibid [258].

101   Ian Sample, 'Even Basic Phone Logs Can Reveal Deeply Personal Information, Researchers Find', The Guardian, 16 May 2016, https://www.theguardian.com/science/2016/may/16/even-basic-phone-logs-can- reveal-deeply-personal-information-researchers-find.

102   Tele2 Sverige AB, judgment (n 29) [101]. See also Digital Rights Ireland (n 73) [28].

103   See, further, Sidhu (n 79).

104   This is particularly true in relation to the significantly reduced resource implications associated with digital sur- veillance, compared with other techniques.

105   Carpenter v United States (n 43) 12.

106   ibid 13.

107   Intelligence and Security Committee of Parliament (UK), 'Privacy and Security: A Modern and Transparent Legal Framework', HC 1075, 12 March 2015, para 80.

108   ECtHR, Tagayeva and Others v Russia, Judgment, App nos 26562/07, 49380/08, 21294/11, 37096/11, 14755/08, 49339/08 and 51313/08, Judgment, 13 April 2017, para 482.

109   ibid.

110   Case C-362/14 Maximillian Schrems v Data Protection Commissioner, Judgment, 6 October 2015, ECLI:EU: C:2015:650, [94].

111   Digital Rights Ireland (n 73) [39].

112   Davis and Others v Secretary of State for the Home Department (n 13).

113   See Marko Milanovic, 'Human Rights Treaties and Foreign Surveillance: Privacy in the Digital Age' (2015) 56 Harvard International Law Journal 81, 141.

114   Tele2 Sverige AB, AG Opinion (n 19) [259].

115   See Intelligence and Security Committee of Parliament (UK) (n 107) para 80.

116   Szabo and Vissy v Hungary (n 5) para 70.

117   ECtHR, Big Brother Watch and Others v United Kingdom, App nos 58170/13, 62322/14 and 24960/15,13 September 2018, para 356.

118   Carpenter v United States (n 43)

119   Maximillian Schrems v Data Protection Commissioner (n 110) [94].

120   Digital Rights Ireland (n 73) [93].

121   Maximillian Schrems v Data Protection Commissioner (n 110) [93].

122   Big Brother Watch and Others v United Kingdom (n 117) paras 328–47.

123   Szabo and Vissy v Hungary (n 5) para 73.

124   Tele2 Sverige AB, judgment (n 29) [102].

125   See Joined Cases C-465/00, C-138/01 and C-139/01 Rechnungshof v Osterreichischer Rundfunk and Others, Judgment, 20 May 2003, ECLI:EU:C:2003:294, [71].

126 Investigatory Powers Act 2016 (n 2) s 263.

127 It is noted that the CJEU effectively invalidated elements of the UK Investigatory Powers Act where access to retained communications data was for purposes deemed to fall short of 'serious crime'. The UK government must now present changes, and put amendments to the legislation before Parliament: Tele2 Sverige AB, judgment (n 29) [125]; Consultation Outcome: Investigatory Powers Act 2016, GOV.UK, 30 November 2017, https://www.gov.uk/ government/ consultations/investigatory-powers-act-2016.

128 ECtHR, Centrum för Rättvisa v Sweden, App no 35252/08, 19 June 2018, para 112.

129 Big Brother Watch and Others v United Kingdom (n 117) para 314.

130 Szabo and Vissy v Hungary (n 5) para 77; ECtHR, Zakharov v Russia, App no 47173/06, 4 December 2015, para 233.

131 This was discussed in Big Brother Watch and Others (n 117): see conclusions reached at para 387.

132 The role of the Investigatory Powers Commission in this regard is interesting, and although it is too early to reach a conclusion, this body may provide insight into how effective oversight in a national security context   may be conducted.

Chapter 5: Germany's Intelligence Reform: More Surveillance, Modest Restraints and Inefficient Controls. Thorsten Wetzling

1 The Bundestag amended both the foreign intelligence agency act (Gesetz über den Bundesnachrichtendienst, hereafter: BND Law) and the law on parliamentary intelligence oversight (Gesetz über die parlamentarische Kontrolle nachrichtendienstlicher Tätigkeit des Bundes). Unfortunately, since the reform there have been no official translations of both laws into English.

2 Next to 16 intelligence services at the state level, Germany has two other federal intelligence services: the Bundesverfassungsschutz (domestic intelligence service) and the Militärischer Abschirmdienst (military intelligence).

3 Notice also that the so-called foreign-foreign traffic may still be transitioning through German internet hubs and, consequently, accessed by Germany's foreign intelligence service on domestic territory.

4   Other existing statutes such as the act on parliamentary intelligence oversight (PKGr Law) as well as the acts on the domestic and the military intelligence service and additional laws regulating to the vetting and classification procedures are of minor relevance for this paper.

5   For individual and strategic measures under Art. 10 Law.

6   For strategic surveillance measures under the BND Law.

7   See Section 15.6 Art. 10 Law for foreign-domestic strategic surveillance or Sections 9.4 or Sections 9.5 BND LAW for foreign-foreign strategic surveillance, respectively.

8   Prior to the 2016 reform, the German government justified the legality of the BND's foreign-foreign strategic surveillance practice with a broad provision in the BND Law according to which "the Federal Intelligence Service shall collect and analyze information required for obtaining foreign intelligence, which is of importance for the foreign and security policy of the Federal Republic of Germany" (Section 1.2).

9   For more information on a these legal theories, including the so-called Weltraumtheorie (space theory), Funktionsträgertheorie (functionary theory), see (Biermann 2014; von Notz 2017).

10 Note that Section 6.4 of the BND Law explicitly excludes national data from strategic foreign-foreign surveillance. Due to widespread doubts on the technical feasibility to ensure this protection in practice, the NSA-inquiry committee summoned expert opinions from an IT-security Professor at the University of the Armed Forces and from the Chaos Computer Club. They elaborated on the accuracy of modern geolocation filtering and both reports indicate that a 100 per cent success may only be approximated. See the reports https://cdn. netzpolitik.org/wp-upload/2016/10/gutachten_ip_lokalisation_rodosek.pdf and www.ccc. de/system/uploads/220/original/beweisbeschluss-nsaua-ccc.pdf

11 In every single legislative period over the last decade, the Bundestag established an ad hoc inquiry into allegations of intelligence governance malfeasance. While those proceedings were doubtlessly politicized, they did provide enough material to show that the permanent intelligence oversight mechanisms were neither sufficient nor fit for purpose (Wetzling 2016a).

12 Their lobbying was strong and briefly put the entire reform effort on halt in the spring of 2016. https://www.welt.de/politik/deutschland/

article153455819/Kanzleramt-legt-BND-Reform-vorerst-auf-Eis.
html

13 A detailed review of each of those cases goes beyond the scope of this paper. The biggest internet hub in Germany (DE-Cix) sued the government in a pending case over the legality of surveillance orders. The G10 Commission lost a case against the government for access to the so-called NSA-selectors. The qualified minority lost a case against the government on an access to information request. NGOs such as Reporters without Borders, Amnesty International and Gesellschaft für Freiheitsrechte have also sued the government over the constitutionality of its surveillance practices.

14 The government referred to "technical and organizational deficits at the BND that the Chancellery identified as part of its executive control" (Frankfurter Allgemeine Zeitung, 23.04.2015). Given that the Chancellery failed to provide clear briefing for SIGINT staffers on German strategic interests and the risks of too credulous intelligence cooperation, a more critical self-assessment of executive control would have been in order, too.

15 At the time of writing this has not been achieved and important positions have yet to be filled. For example, the new secretariat of the parliamentary intelligence oversight body (PK1-Bundestagsverwaltung) has yet to appear on the organization chart of the Bundestag administration and new positions (e.g. Leitender Beamter, Section 12.1 PKrG Law) have yet to be filled.

16 See (Deutscher Bundestag 2016) for a comprehensive list of individual expert reports on the draft BND-reform.

17 Section 20.1 BNDG in conjunction with Section 12 BVerfSchG.

18 Unless otherwise indicated, all references to sections in this text refer to the BND Law.

19 See (Graulich 2017:49).

20 Note: The purely "foreign" strategic surveillance practice by the BND, i.e. the collection of foreigners' data on foreign soil remains unregulated. This will be further explained in the analysis part.

21 For a good overview, see the comparative study on European SIGINT laws by the European Fundamental Rights Agency: Surveillance by Intelligence Services: fundamental rights safeguards and remedies in the EU, November 2015.http://fra.europa.eu/en/publication/2015/surveillance-intelligence-services.

22 In October 2015, the G10 Commission sued the government over access to NSA-selectors. Irrespective of the merits of this unsuccessful case for the G10 Commission, it is safe to assume that the very fact that the Commission turned to the Constitutional Court has tarnished the Chancellery's trust in the Commission's four honorary fellows.

23 This particular provision stems from the pre-digital era and is highly problematic and amenable to frequent abuse. See (Wetzling 2016) for a further elaboration. Given that the reform stayed clear from any changes to the existing Art. 10 Law, this problem remains.

24 Implementation Plan for the Principles for Intelligence Transparency. Available at https:// www.dni.gov/files/documents/Newsroom/ Reports%20and%20Pubs/Principles%20of%20   Intelligence%20 Transparency%20Implementation%20Plan.pdf

25 See the 2015 Annual G10 Report by the Parliamentary Intelligence Oversight Body.

26 See Wetzling 2016 for further elaboration on those deficits.

27 Eckpunktepapier SPD Party (June 2015), available online: http:// www.spdfraktion.de/   system/files/documents/2015-06-16-eck-punkte_reform_strafma-r-endfassung.pdf

28 For an English translation of this announcement, see: https://blog. cyberwar.nl/2017/04/ dutch-review-committee-on-the-intelligence-security-services-ctivd-to-self-assess-effectiveness-of-lawfulness-oversight-re-large-scale-data-intensive-a/

29 By way of comparison, take a hypothetical scenario discussed in (Martin, 2017): In 2015, the data volume carried only be broadband connection in Germany amounted to roughly 11.500 million gigabyte. If only five percent of this data would not be properly filtered that would mean that 575 million gigabyte of data would not be subject to proper data minimization. A standard article like this one may amount to 0.00005 gigabyte. Put differently, and referring still to the hypothetical example, 11 trillion and 500 billion data set would not be subjected to proper data protection standards required by law.

30 For example, the new secretariat of the parliamentary intelligence oversight body (PK1- Bundestagsverwaltung) has yet to appear on the organization chart of the Bundestag administration and new positions (e.g. Leitender Beamter, Section 12.1 PKrG Law) have yet to be filled.

31   To be fair, the U.S. Privacy and Civil Liberties Board (PCLOB) – currently operating its important business with only one member – may also make recommendations designed to protect the rights for non-U.S. persons.

Bibliography

Backer, Matthias. 2014. Erhebung, Bevorratung und Übermittlung von Telekommunikationsdaten durch die Nachrichtendienste des Bundes. Stellungnahme zur Anhörung des NSA-Untersuchungsausschusses. 22.Mai 2014. Available at www.bundestag.de.

Biermann, Kai. 2014. Die Anarchos vom BND. Commentary for Zeit Online. Availableathttp://www.zeit.de/politik/deutschland/2014-11/bnd-   bundesnachrichtendienst-gesetz-grundrecht

Born, Hans and Leigh, Ian. 2002. Making Intelligence Accountable: Legal Standards and Best Practices for Oversight of Intelligence Agencies. (Oslo: Norwegian Parliament Press). Available at www.dcaf.ch

Deutscher Bundestag. 2016. Statements by Gärditz, Graulich, Wetzling, Schindler, Töpfer, Wolff and Bäcker on the draft intelligence reform. Ausschussdrucksachen 18(4)653 A-G. Available at: ww.bundestag.de/inneres

Deutscher Bundestag. 2015. Annual report on surveillance measures by the federal intelligence agencies under Art. 10 Law. Drucksache 18/3709. Available at www. bundestag.de

Garditz, Klaus. 2017. Legal Restraints on the Extraterritorial Activities of Germany's Intelligence Services. in: Miller, Russell (ed.). 2017. Privacy and Power: A transatlantic dialogue in the shadows of the NSA-affair. (Cambridge: Cambridge University Press).

Graulich, Kurt. 2017. Reform des Gesetzes über den Bundesnachrichtendienst.Kriminalpolitische Zeitschrift 2:1, 43-52.

Heumann, Stefan. 2017. German exceptionalism? The Debate about the German Foreign Intelligence Service (BND) in: Miller, Russell (ed.). 2017. Privacy and Power: A transatlantic dialogue in the shadows of the NSA-affair. (Cambridge: Cambridge University Press).

Hofmann-Riem, Wolfgang. 2015. Legal protection against surveillance by intelligence agencies:On the need for its reform. Bucerius Law Journal 2/2015 44-50. Available here: http://www.law-school.de/

Martin, Stephan. 2017. Snowden und die Folgen. Infobrief 113/2017. RAV Berlin. Available at http://www.rav.de/publikationen/infobriefe/ infobrief-113-2017/ snowden-und-die-folgen/

Meister, Andre. 2016. Secret Report: German Federal Intelligence Service BND violates laws and constitution by the dozen. Available at: https://cryptome. org/2016/09/de-nixes-xkeyscore-netzpolitik-16-0902.pdf

Loffelmann, Markus. 2015. Regelung der Routineaufklärung. Recht + Politik, Volume 6:2015. Available at: http://www.recht-politik.de/ regelung-der-%E2%80%9Eroutineaufklarung/

Papier, Hans-Jürgen. 2017. Strategische Fernmeldeüberwachung durch den Bundesnachrichtendienst. Deutsche Richterzeitung 01/17, 17-23.

Topfer, Eric. Kooperation im kontrollfreien Raum: Zur aktuellen Entgrenzung der Geheimdienste. Infobrief 113/2017. RAV Berlin. Available at: www.rav.de/ publikationen/infobriefe/ infobrief-113-2017/kooperation-im-kontrollfreien- raum/

Von Notz, Konstantin. 2017. The Challenges of Limiting Intelligence Agencies' Mass Surveillance Regimes: Why Western Democracies Cannot gives up on Communication Privacy. in: Miller, Russell (ed.). 2017. Privacy and Power: A transatlantic dialogue in the shadows of the NSA-affair. (Cambridge: Cambridge University Press).

Wetzling, Thorsten. 2016. The key to intelligence reform in Germany: Strengthening the G10-Commission's role to authorize strategic surveillance. Policy Brief 02/16. Stiftung Neue Verantwortung, Berlin. Available at: www.stiftung-nv.de

Wetzling, Thorsten. 2016a. Aufklärung ohne Aufsicht? Über die Leistungsfähigkeit der Nachrichtendienstkontrolle in Deutschland. Band 43/Demokratie. Heinrich- Böll-Stiftung, Berlin. Available at: www.boell.de

Chapter 6: Theorizing Surveillance in the UK Crime Control Field. Michael McCahill

Alhadar, I., & McCahill, M. (2011). The use of surveil-lance cameras in a Riyadh shopping mall. Theoretical Criminology, 15(3), 315-330.

Ball, K., & Webster, W. (2003). The intensification of sur-veillance. In K. Ball & F. Webster (Eds.), The intensifi-cation of surveillance: Crime, terrorism and warfare in the information age. (pp. 1-15). London: Pluto Press

Ball, K., Canhoto, A., Daniel, E., Dibb, S., Meadows, M., & Spiller, K. (2015). The private security State. Freder-iksberg: CBS Press.

Bennett, C. J., Haggerty, K. D., Lyon, D., & Steeves, V. (2014). Transparent lives: Surveillance in Canada. Athabasca University: Athabasca University Press.

Bennett, T., Savage, M., Silva, E., Warde, A., Gayo-Cal, M., & Wright, D. (2010). Culture, class, distinction. London: Routledge.

Benson, R. (2005). Mapping field variation: Journalism in France and the United States. In R. Benson & E. Neveu (Eds.), Bourdieu and the journalistic field (pp. 85-112). Cambridge: Polity Press.

Bigo, D. (2000). Liaison officers in Europe: New officers in the European security field. In J. W. E. Sheptycki (Ed.), Issues in transnational policing (pp. 67-99). London: Routledge.

Bigo, D. (2002). Security and immigration: Toward a cri-tique of the governmentality of unease. Alternatives, 27(1), 63-92.

Bogard, W. (2006). Surveillance assemblages and lines of flight. In D. Lyon (Ed.), Theorizing surveillance: The panopticon and beyond (pp. 97-122). Cullompton: Willan.

Bogard, W. (2012). Simulation and post-panopticism. In K. Ball, K. Haggertyand, & D. Lyon (Eds.), Routledge handbook of surveillance studies (pp. 3-37). Abing-don: Routledge.

Bourdieu, P. (1977). Outline of a theory of practice. Cambridge: Cambridge University Press.

Bourdieu, P. (1984). Rethinking the State: Genesis and structure of the bureaucratic field. Sociological Theo-ry, 12(1), 1-18.

Bourdieu, P. (1990). In other words: Essays towards a re-Media and Communication, 2015, Volume 3, Issue 2, Pages 10-20 19 flexive sociology. Cambridge: Polity Press.

Bourdieu, P. (1991). Language and symbolic power. Cambridge: Harvard University Press.

Bourdieu, P. (1998). Acts of resistance against the new myths of our times. Cambridge: Polity Press.

Bourdieu, P. (2005). The social structures of the econo-my. Cambridge: Polity Press.

Bourdieu, P., & Wacquant, L. (1992). An invitation to re-flexive sociology. Chicago: University of Chicago Press.

Bozbeyoglu, A. C. (2012). The electronic eye of the po-lice: The provincial information and security system in Istanbul. In A. Doyle, R. Lippert, & D. Lyon (Eds.), Eyes everywhere: The global growth of camera surveillance (pp. 139-155). London: Routledge.

Cavadino, M., & Dignan, J. (2006). Penal systems: a comparative approach. London: Sage.

Coleman, R. (2004). Reclaiming the streets: Surveillance, social control and the city. Cullompton: Willan.

Couzens Hoy, D. (2005). Critical resistance: From post-structuralism to post-critique. Massachusetts: MIT Press.

Dandeker, C. (1990). Surveillance, power and modernity: Bureaucracy and discipline from 1700 to the present day. Cambridge: Polity Press.

Deleuze, G. (1992). Postscript on the societies of control. October, 59, 3-7.

Doyle, A., Lippert, R., & Lyon, D. (2012). Introduction. In A. Doyle, R. Lippert, & D. Lyon (Eds.) Eyes every-where: The global growth of camera surveillance (pp. 1-19). London: Routledge.

Dupont, B. (2004). Security in the age of networks. Polic-ing and Society, 14(1), 76-91.

Feeley, M., & Simon, J. (1992). The new penology. Crimi-nology, 30(4), 449-474.

Foucault, M. (1977). Discipline and punish: The birth of the prison. London: Allen Lane.

Foucault, M. (2001). Interview with Michel Foucault. In J. D. Faubion (Ed.), Essential works of Foucault 1954–1984, Volume 3; Power. London: Penguin Books.

Garland, D. (2001). The culture of control: Crime and so-cial order in contemporary society. Oxford: OUP.

Giddens, A. (1985). The nation state and violence: Volume two of a contemporary critique of historical ma-terialism. Cambridge: Polity Press.

Gilliom, J. (2001). Overseers of the poor: Surveillance and the limits of privacy. Chicago: University of Chicago Press.

Gilliom, J., & Monahan, T. (2012). Everyday Resistance. In K. Ball, K. D. Haggerty, & D. Lyon (Eds.), Routledge handbook of surveillance studies (pp. 405-11). Abingdon: Routledge.

Haggerty, K. D. (2004). Displaced expertise: Three con-straints on the policy-relevance of criminological thought. Theoretical Criminology, 8(2), 211-231.

Haggerty, K. D. (2006). Tear down the walls: On demolishing the panopticon. In D. Lyon (Ed.), Theorizing surveillance: The panopticon and beyond (pp. 23-45). Cullompton: Willan.

Haggerty, K. D., & Ericson, R. V. (2000). The surveillant assemblage. British Journal of Sociology, 51(4), 605-622.

Haggerty, K. D., & Ericson, R. V. (2006). The new politics of surveillance and visibility. In K. D. Haggerty & R. V. Ericson (Eds.), The new politics of surveillance and visibility (pp. 3-25). Toronto: University of Toronto Press.

Johnston, L., & Shearing, C. (2003). Governing security: Explorations in policing and justice. London: Routledge.

Kemshall, H., & Maguire, M. (2001). Public protection, partnership and risk penalty: The multi-agency risk management of sexual and violent offenders. Pun-ishment and Society, 3(2), 237-264.

Lacey, N. (2008). The prisoners' dilemma: political econ-omy and punishment in contemporary democracies. Cambridge: Cambridge

University Press.

Loveman, M. (2005). The modern State and the primitive accumulation of symbolic power. American Journal of Sociology, 110(6), 1651-1683.

Luke, S. (2005). Power: A radical view. Basingstoke: Pal-grave Macmillan.

Lyon, D. (1993). An electronic panopticon? A sociological critique of surveillance theory. The Sociological Re-view, 41(4), 653-678.

Lyon, D. (1994). The electronic eye: The rise of the surveillance society. Cambridge: Polity Press.

Lyon, D. (2001). Surveillance society: Monitoring every-day life. Buckingham: Open University.

Marx, G. T. (2002). What's new about the new surveillance? Classifying for change and continuity. Surveil-lance and Society, 1(1), 9-29.

Marx, G. T. (2003). A tack in the shoe: Neutralizing and resisting the new surveillance. Journal of Social Is-sues, 59(2), 369-390.

McCahill, M. (2002). The surveillance web: The rise of visual surveillance in an English city. Devon: Willan

McCahill, M., & Finn, R. L. (2014). Surveillance, capital and resistance: Theorizing the surveillance subject. Abingdon: Routledge.

McNay, L. (2000). Gender and agency: Reconfiguring the subject in feminist and social theory. Cambridge: Poli-ty.

Minnaar, A. (2012). The growth and further proliferation of camera surveillance in South Africa. In A. Doyle, R. Lippert, & D. Lyon (Eds.), Eyes everywhere: The global growth of camera surveillance (pp. 100-121). Lon-don: Routledge.

Murakami Wood, D. (2009). The surveillance society: Questions of history, place and culture. European Journal of Criminology, 6(2), 179-194.

Murakami Wood, D. (2012). Cameras in context: A com-parison of the place of video surveillance in Japan and Brazil. In A. Doyle, R. Lippert, & D. Lyon (Eds.), Media and Communication, 2015, Volume 3, Issue 2, Pages 10-20 20

Murakami Wood, D., & Webster, W. (2009). Living in surveillance societies: The normalization of surveil-lance in Europe. Journal of Contemporary European Research, 5(2), 259-273.

Nayak, A. (2006). Displaced masculinities: chavs, youth and class in the post-industrial city. Sociology, 40(5), 813-831.

Nelken, D. (2005). When is a society non-punitive? The Italian case. In J. Pratt, M. Brown, S. Hallsworth, & W. Morrison (Eds.), The new punitiveness: Trends, theo-ries, perspectives (pp. 218-238). Cullompton: Willan.

Norris, C. (2003). From personal to digital: CCTV, the panopticon, and the technological mediation of sus-picion and social control. In D. Lyon (Ed.), Surveil-lance as social sorting: Privacy, risk and digital dis-crimination (pp. 249-281). New York: Routledge.

Norris, C. (2007). The intensification and bifurcation of surveillance in British criminal justice policy. European Journal on Criminal Policy and Research, 13(1–2), 139-158.

Norris, C. (2012). The success of failure: Accounting for the global growth of CCTV. In K. Ball, K. Haggerty, & D. Lyon (Eds.), Routledge handbook of surveillance studies (pp. 251-58). Abingdon: Routledge.

Norris, C., & Armstrong, G. (1999). The maximum surveillance society. Oxford: Berg.

Norris, C., McCahill, M., & Murakami Wood, D. (2004). The growth of CCTV: A global perspective on the international diffusion of video surveillance in publicly accessible space. Surveillance and Society, 2(2–3), 110-135. Retrieved from www.surveillance-andsociety.org

Page, J. (2013). Punishment and the penal field. In J. Si-mon & R. Sparks (Eds.), The Sage handbook of pun-ishment and society (pp. 152-166). London: Sage.

Scott, A. (2013). We are the State: Pierre Bourdieu on the State and the Political Field. Rivista di Storia Idee, 2(1), 56-70. Retrieved from http://www.academia.   edu/4296007/We_are_the_state._Pierre_Bourdieu_on_the_state_and_political_field

Scott, J. C. (1990). Domination and the arts of resistance: Hidden transcripts. New Haven: Yale University Press.

Shilling, C. (2003). The body and social theory. London: Sage.

Simon, J. (2007). Governing through crime. Oxford: OUP.

Smith, G. J. D. (2015). Opening the black box: The work of watching. London: Routledge.

Staples, W. G., & Decker, S. K. (2008). Technologies of the body, technologies of the self: House arrest as neo-liberal governance. In M. Deflem (Ed.), Surveillance and governance: Crime control and beyond (pp. 131-149). Bingley: Emerald Group Publishing Limited.

Sutton, A., & Wilson, D. (2004). Open-street CCTV in Australia: The politics of resistance and expansion. Surveillance and Society, 2(2–3), 310-322.

Swartz, D. L. (2004). The State as the central bank of symbolic credit. Paper presented at the American So-ciological Association 99th Annual Meeting, August 14–17, 2004, San Francisco, USA. Retrieved from http://people.bu.edu/dswartz/articles/10.html

Thompson, J. B. (1991). Editors introduction. In P. Bour-dieu (Ed.), Language and symbolic power (pp. 1-31). Cambridge: Polity Press.

Wacquant, L. (1993). From ruling class to field of power: An interview with Pierre Bourdieu. La Noblesse d'Etat, Theory, Culture and Society, 10(3), 19-44.

Wacquant, L. (2005). Symbolic power in the rule of the state nobility. In W. Wacquant (Ed.), Bourdieu and democratic politics. Cambridge: Polity Press.

Wacquant, L. (2009a). Punishing the poor: The neoliberal government of social insecurity. Durham and London: Duke University Press.

Wacquant, L. (2009b). The body, the ghetto and the pe-nal State. Qualitative Sociology, 32(1), 101-129.

Wacquant, L. (2010). Crafting the neoliberal State: Work-fare, prisonfare, and social insecurity. Sociological Forum, 25(2), 197-220.

Wakefield, A. (2003). Selling security: The private policing of public space. Cullompton: Willan.

About the Author Dr. Michael McCahill

Chapter 7: Artificial Intelligence Governance and Ethics: Global Perspectives. Angela Daly, Thilo Hagendorff, Li Hui, Monique Mann, Vidushi Marda, Ben Wagner, Wei Wang and Saskia Witteborn

All-Party Parliamentary Group on Artificial Intelligence (APPG AI). (n.d.). Retrieved from: https://www.appg-i.org/

Arkin, R. (2009). Ethical robots in warfare,IEEE Technology&SocietyMa gazine,28(1),3033.doi:10.1109/MTS.2009.931858

Australian Government Department of Industry, Innovation and Science. (2019). Artificial intelligence: Australia's ethics framework. Retrieved from: https://consult.industry.gov.au/strategic-policy/ artificial-intelligence-ethics-framework/

Australian Human Rights Commission. (2018). Human rights and technology. Retrieved from: https://www.humanrights.gov.au/our-work/rights-and-freedoms/projects/human-rights-andtechnology

Beijing Academy of Artificial Intelligence. (2019). Beijing AI principles. Retrieved from: http://www.baai.ac.cn/blog/beijing-ai-principles.

Bundesministerium für Bildung und Forschung, Bundesministerium für Wirtschaft und Energie, & Bundesministerium für Arbeit und Soziales. (2018). Strategie künstliche intelligenz der bundesregierung. Retrieved from: https://www.bmwi. de/Redaktion/DE/Publikationen/Technologie/strategie-kuenstlicheintelligenz-der-bundesregierung.html

Bundesministerium Verkehr, Innovation und Technologie and Bundesministerium Digitalisierung und Wirtschaftsstandort. AIM at 2030: Artificial Intelligence Mission Austria 2030. Retrieved from: https://www.bmvit.gv.at/innovation/publikationen/ikt/ downloads/aimat_ua.pdf

Calo, R. (2015). Robotics and the lessons of cyber law. California Law Review, 103(3), 513-63. doi:10.2139/ssrn.2402972

Cave, S. & Óh Éigeartaigh, S. (2018). An AI Race for Strategic Advantage: Rhetoric and Risks. Paper presented at AI Ethics And Society Conference, New Orleans, USA. Retrieved from: http://www.aies-conference.com/wp-content/papers/main/AIES_2018_paper_163. pdf

China Daily. (2019). Governance principles for the new generation Artificial Intelligence--Developing responsible Artificial Intelligence. Retrieved from: http://www.chinadaily.com.cn/a/201906/17/WS5d07486ba3103dbf14328ab7.html?from=groupmessage&isappinstalled=0

Cisse, M. (2018). Look to Africa to advance Artificial Intelligence. Nature, 562(7728), 461. doi:10.1038/d41586-018-07104-7

Consultative Committee of the Convention for the Protection of Individuals with regard to Automatic Processing of Personal Data (Convention 108). (2019). Guidelines on Artificial Intelligence and data protection. Retrieved from: https://rm.coe.int/guidelines-on-artificial-intelligenceand-data-protection/168091f9d8 Council of Europe. (n.d.).

Council of Europe and Artificial Intelligence. Retrieved from: https://www.coe.int/en/web/artificial-intelligence

Delcker, J. (2018). US, Russia block formal talks on whether to ban 'killer robots'. Politico. Retrieved from: https://www.politico.eu/article/killer-robots-us-russia-block-formal-talks-on-whether-toban/ DeepMind. (n.d.). Ethics and society principles. Retrieved from: https://deepmind.com/applied/deepmind-ethics-society/principles/

Edwards, L. & Veale, M. (2017). Slave to the algorithm? Why a 'right to an explanation' is probably not the remedy you are looking for. Duke Law & Technology Review, 16(1), 18-84. doi:10.2139/ssrn.2972855

ELRC. (2019). Artificial Intelligence: An evangelical statement of principles. Retrieved from: https://erlc.com/resource-library/statements/artificial-intelligence-an-evangelical-statementof-principles

European Commission. (2018). European group on ethics in science and new technologies statement on Artificial Intelligence, robotics and 'autonomous' systems. Retrieved from: https://ec.europa.eu/research/ege/pdf/ege_ai_statement_2018.pdf

European Commission Independent High-Level Expert Group on Artificial Intelligence. (2019a). Ethics Guidelines for Trustworthy AI. Final Report. Retrieved from: https://ec.europa.eu/digital-single-market/en/news/ethics-guidelines-trustworthy-ai

European Commission Independent High-Level Expert Group on Artificial Intelligence. (2019b). Policy and Investment Recommendations for Trustworthy AI. Retrieved from: https://ec.europa.eu/digital-single-market/en/news/policy-and-investment-recommendationstrustworthy-artificial-intelligence

European Commission for the Administration of Justice (CEPEJ). (2018). European ethical charter on the use of Artificial Intelligence in judicial systems and their environment. Retrieved from: https://rm.coe.int/ethical-charter-en-for-publication-4-december-2018/16808f699c

European Group on Ethics in Science and New Technologies. (2018). Statement on Artificial Intelligence, robotics and 'autonomous systems'. Retrieved from: https://ec.europa.eu/research/ege/pdf/ege_ai_statement_2018.pdf

European Parliament. (2017). Resolution of 16 February 2017 with recommendations to the Commission on Civil Law Rules on Robotics (2015/2103(INL)). Retrievedfrom:https://eurlex.europa.eu/legal-content/EN/TXT/HTML/?uri=CELEX:32016R0679&from=EN#d1e2793-1

Ferguson, A.G. (2017). The rise of big data policing: Surveillance, race and the future of law enforcement. New York: NYU Press.

FLIA. (2017). China's new generation of Artificial Intelligence development plan. English translation. Retrieved from: https://flia.org/notice-state-council-issuing-new-generation-artificialintelligence-development-plan/

Future of Life Institute (2017). Asilomar AI principles. Retrieved from: https://futureoflife.org/aiprinciples/

G20. (2019). Ministerial statement on trade and digital economy. Retrieved from: https://g20tradedigital.go.jp/dl/Ministerial_Statement_on_Trade_and_Digital_Economy.pdf

Government of India Ministry of Commerce and Industry. (2018). Report of the Artificial Intelligence Task Force. Retrieved from: https://dipp.gov.in/sites/default/files/Report_of_Task_Force_on_ArtificialIntelligence_20Marc h2018_2.pdf

Government of India Ministry of Electronics & Information Technology. (n.d.). Digital India programme. Retrieved from: https://

digitalindia.gov.in/

Government of India Ministry of Finance. (n.d.). Make in India. Retrieved from: www.makeinindia.com/home/

Government of India Ministry of Housing and Urban Affairs. (n.d.). Smart Cities Mission. Retrieved from: http://www.smartcities.gov. in/content/

Hagendorff, T. (2019). The ethics of AI ethics. An evaluation of guidelines. arXiv, 1–15.

Hildebrandt, M. (2008). Defining profiling: A new type of knowledge? In M. Hildebrandt & S. Gutwirth (Eds.), Profiling the European citizen: Cross-disciplinary perspectives (pp.17-45). Dordrecht: Springer.

Höffe, O. (2013). Ethik: Eine einführung. München: C. H. Beck.

Hong Kong Monetary Authority. (2019). Use of personal data in Fintech development. Retrieved from: https://www. hkma.gov.hk/media/eng/doc/key-information/guidelines-andcircular/2019/20190503e1.pdf

House of Lords Select Committee on Artificial Intelligence. (2018). AI in the UK: Ready, willing, able? Retrieved from: https://publications. parliament.uk/pa/ld201719/ldselect/ldai/100/100.pdf

ICDPPC. (2018). Declaration on Ethics and Data Protection in Artificial Intelligence. Retrieved from: https://icdppc.org/wp-content/ uploads/2018/10/20180922_ICDPPC-40th_AIDeclaration_ ADOPTED.pdf

IEEE. (2018). Global initiative on ethics of autonomous and intelligent systems - Ethically aligned design, version 2. Retrieved from: https://standards.ieee.org/content/dam/ieeestandards/standards/ web/documents/other/ead_v2.pdf

Indigenous AI. (n.d.). Retrieved from: http://www.indigenous-ai.net/

ITU. (2018). United Nations activities on Artificial Intelligence. Retrieved from: https://www.itu.int/dms_pub/itu-s/opb/gen/S-GEN-UNACT-2018-1-PDF-E.pdf

Koizumi, M. (2019). G20 ministers agree on guiding principles for using artificial intelligence. Japan Times. Retrieved from: https://www.

japantimes.co.jp/news/2019/06/08/business/g20ministers-kick-talks-trade-digital-economy-ibaraki-prefecture/#.XRB3zY8RU2w

Laskai, L. & Webster, G. (2019). Translation: Chinese expert group offers 'governance principles' for 'responsible AI'. New America Foundation. Retrieved from: https://www.newamerica.org/cybersecurity-initiative/digichina/blog/translation-chineseexpert-group-offers-governance-principles-responsible-ai/

Leenes, R. & Lucivero, F. (2014). Laws on robots, laws by robots, laws in robots: Regulating robot behaviour by design. Law, Innovation & Technology, 6(2), 193-220. doi:10.5235/17579961.6.2.193

Marda, V. (2018). Artificial Intelligence Policy in India: A Framework for Engaging the Limits of DataDriven Decision-Making. Philosophical Transactions of the Royal Society A: Mathematical, Physical and Engineering Sciences, 376(2133).

Mason, R. (2017). Four ethical issues of the information age. In J. Wekert (Ed.), Computer ethics (pp. 41-8). London: Routledge.

Metzinger, T. (2019). EU guidelines: Ethics washing made in Europe. Der Tagesspeigel. Retrieved from: https://www.tagesspiegel.de/politik/eu-guidelines-ethics-washing-made-ineurope/24195496.html

Microsoft. (n.d.). Our approach to AI. Retrieved from: https://www.microsoft.com/en-us/AI/ourapproach-to-ai

Mittelstadt, B. (2019). AI Ethics –Too principled to fail? Retrieved from: https://ssrn.com/abstract=3391293

National Institute for Science and Technology. (2019). NIST requests information on Artificial Intelligence technical standards and tools. Retrieved from: https://www.nist.gov/newsevents/news/2019/05/nist-requests-information-artificial-intelligence-technical-standards-and

NITI Aayog. (2018). National strategy for Artificial Intelligence. Discussion paper. Retrieved from: https://niti.gov.in/writereaddata/files/document_publication/NationalStrategy-for-AIDiscussion-Paper.pdf

OECD. (2019). OECD Principles on AI. Retrieved from: https://www.oecd.org/goingdigital/ai/principles/

O'Neil, C. (2016). Weapons of math destruction: How big data increases inequality and threatens democracy. UK: Penguin, Random House.

Open AI. (2018). Open AI Charter. Retrieved from: https://openai.com/charter/ Partnership on AI. (n.d.). Tenets. Retrieved from: https://www.partnershiponai.org/tenets/

Office of the Victorian Information Commissioner. (2018). Artificial Intelligence and privacy. Issues paper. Retrieved from: https://ovic.vic.gov.au/wp-content/uploads/2018/08/AI-Issues-PaperV1.1.pdf

Pekka, AP, Bauer, W., Bergmann, U., Bieliková, M., Bonefeld-Dahl, C., Bonnet, Y. et al. (2018). The European Commission's High-Level Expert Group on Artificial Intelligence. Ethics guidelines for trustworthy AI. Working document for stakeholders' consultation. Retrieved from: https://www.euractiv.com/wpcontent/uploads/sites/2/2018/12/AIHLEGDraftAIEthicsGuidelinespdf.pdf

Pichai, S. (2018). AI at Google: Our principles. Retrieved from: https://www.blog.google/technology/ai/ai-principles/

Pressman, A. & Lashinsky, A. (2019). Data sheet—Trump's smart move on Artificial Intelligence. Fortune. Retrieved from: http://fortune.com/2019/05/28/data-sheet-trump-artificialintelligence-oecd/

Privacy Commissioner for Personal Data, Hong Kong. (2018). Ethical accountability framework for Hong Kong, China: Analysis and model assessment framework. Retrieved from: https://www.pcpd.org.hk/misc/files/Ethical_Accountability_Framework.pdf

Rahwan, I., Cebrian, M., Obradovich, N., Bongard, J., Bonnefon, JF, Breazeal, C. et al. (2019). Machine behaviour. Nature, 568(7753), 477–486. doi:10.1038/s41586-019-1138-y

Russo, A. (2018). United Kingdom partners with World Economic Forum to develop first Artificial Intelligence procurement policy. World Economic Forum. Retrieved from: https://www.weforum.org/press/2018/09/united-kingdom-partners-with-world-economicforum-to-develop-first-artificial-intelligence-procurement-policy/

Salinger, A. (2019). The ethics of artificial intelligence: start with the law. Salinger Privacy. Retrieved from: https://www.salingerprivacy.com.au/2019/04/27/ai-ethics/

Sandler, R. (2019). San Francisco bans facial recognition technology. Forbes. Retrieved from: https://www.forbes.com/sites/

rachelsandler/2019/05/14/san-francisco-about-to-ban-facialrecog
nition/#6740f4ac7b80

Schreurs, W., Hildebrandt, M., Kindt, E., & Vanfleteren, M. (2008).
Cogitas, ergo sum. The role of data protection law and non-
discrimination law in group profiling in the private sector. In M.
Hildebrandt & S. Gutwirth (Eds.), Profiling the European citizen:
Cross-disciplinary perspectives (pp. 241-70). Dordrecht: Springer.

Si, J. (2018). Towards an ethical framework for Artificial
Intelligence. Retrieved from: https://mp.weixin.qq.com/s/_
CbBsrjrTbRkKjUNdmhuqQ

The White House. (2019). Executive order on maintaining American
leadership in Artificial Intelligence. Retrieved from: https://www.
whitehouse.gov/presidential-actions/executiveorder-maintaining-
american-leadership-artificial-intelligence/

Turner, J. (2019). Google disbands AI committee before first meeting.
Tech.Co. Retrieved from: https://tech.co/news/google-disbands-ai-
committee-2019-04

UK Government. (2017). Industrial strategy: Building a Britain fit for
the future. Retrieved from: https://assets.publishing.service.gov.uk/
government/uploads/system/

UK Government Department for Business, Energy & Industrial Strategy
& Department for Digital, Culture, Media & Sport. (2018). AI
sector deal policy paper. Retrieved from: https://www.gov.uk/
government/publications/artificial-intelligence-sector-deal/ai-
sector-deal

US Department of Defense. (2019). Summary of the 2018 Department of
Defense Artificial Intelligence strategy: Harnessing AI to advance
our security and prosperity. Retrieved from: https://media.defense.
gov/2019/Feb/12/2002088963/-1/-1/1/SUMMARY-OF-DOD-
AISTRATEGY.PDF

Wachter, S. & Mittelstadt, B. (2018). A right to reasonable inferences:
Re-thinking data protection law in the age of Big Data and AI.
Oxford Business Law Blog. Retrieved from: https://www.law.ox.ac.
uk/business-law-blog/blog/2018/10/right-reasonable-inferences-
rethinking-data-protection-law-age-big

Wachter, S., Mittelstadt, B., & Floridi, L. (2017a). Transparent, explainable, and accountable AI for robotics. Science Robotics, 2(6). doi:10.1126/scirobotics.aan6080

Wachter, S., Mittelstadt, B., & Floridi, L. (2017b). Why a right to explanation of automated decisionmaking does not exist in the General Data Protection Regulation. International Data Privacy Law, 7(2), 76-99. doi:10.2139/ssrn.2903469

Wagner, B. (2018). Ethics as an escape from regulation: From ethics-washing to ethics-shopping? In M. Hildebrandt (Ed.), Being profiling. Cogitas ergo sum. Amsterdam: Amsterdam University Press.

Walker, D. (2018). UK gov is making a 'massive strategic error' on AI funding. IT Pro. Retrieved from: https://www.itpro.co.uk/machine-learning/30654/uk-gov-is-making-a-massive-strategicerror-on-ai-funding

Watts, D. (2019). How big tech designs its own rules of ethics to avoid scrutiny and accountability. The Conversation. Retrieved from: https://theconversation.com/how-big-tech-designs-itsown-rules-of-ethics-to-avoid-scrutiny-and-accountability-113457

Webster, G. (2019). Translation: Chinese AI alliance drafts self-discipline 'Joint Pledge'. New America Foundation. Retrieved from: https://www.newamerica.org/cybersecurityinitiative/digichina/blog/translation-chinese-ai-alliance-drafts-self-discipline-joint-pledge/

World Economic Forum. (2019). AI governance: A holistic approach to implement ethics into AI. Retrieved from: https://weforum.my.salesforce.com/sfc/p/#b0000000GycE/a/0X000000cPl1/i.8ZWL2HIR_kA nvckyqVA.nVVgrWIS4LCM1ueGy.gBc

Yu, R. (2017). EADv2 regional reports on A/ISEthics: Hong Kong. Retrieved from: https://standards.ieee.org/content/dam/ieeestandards/standards/web/documents/other/eadv2_regional_report.pdf

Further Resources

Article 19 and Privacy International. (2019). Privacy and Freedom of Expression in the Age of Artificial Intelligence. Retrieved from: https://www.article19.org/wpcontent/uploads/2018/04/Privacy-and-Freedom-of-Expression-In-the-Age-of-ArtificialIntelligence-1.pdf

Article 19. (2019). Governance with Teeth How human rights can strengthen FAT and ethics initiatives on artificial intelligence. Retrieved from: https://www.article19.org/wpcontent/uploads/2019/04/Governance-with-teeth_A19_April_2019.pdf

Algorithms Watch. AI Ethics Guidelines Global Inventory. Retrieved from: https://algorithmwatch.org/en/project/ai-ethics-guidelines-global-inventory/

Arun, C. (2019). AI and the Global South: Designing for Other Worlds. In M. Dubber, F. Pasquale, & S. Das (Eds.), Oxford Handbook of Ethics of Artificial Intelligence. Oxford: Oxford University Press. Retrieved from: https://ssrn.com/abstract=3403010

Daly, A. (2017). Privacy in Automation: An Appraisal of the Emerging Australian Approach. Computer Law & Security Review, 33(6), 836-846.

Daly, A., Devitt, S.K., & Mann, M. (eds). (2019). Good Data. Amsterdam: Institute of Network Cultures. Retrieved from: http://networkcultures.org/blog/publication/tod-29-good-data/

Ebers, M. (2019). Chapter 2: Regulating AI and Robotics: Ethical and Legal Challenges. In M. Ebers & S. Navas Navarro (Eds.), Algorithms and Law. Cambridge: Cambridge University Press, forthcoming. Retrieved from: https://ssrn.com/abstract=3392379

Fjeld, J., Hilligoss, H., Achten, N., Levy Daniel, M., Feldman, J. & Kagay, S. (2019). Principled Artificial Intelligence. Retrieved from: https://ai-hr.cyber.harvard.edu/primp-viz.html

Future of Life. Global AI Policy. Retrieved from: https://futureoflife.org/ai-policy/

Gal, D. (2019). Perspectives and Approaches in AI Ethics: East Asia. In M. Dubber, F. Pasquale, & S. Das (Eds.), Oxford Handbook of Ethics of Artificial Intelligence. Oxford: Oxford University Press. Retrieved from: https://papers.ssrn.com/sol3/papers.cfm?abstract_id=3400816

Latonero, M. (2018). Governing Artificial Intelligence: Upholding Human Rights & Dignity. Data & Society. Retrieved from: https://datasociety.net/wpcontent/uploads/2018/10/   DataSociety_Governing_ Artificial_Intelligence_Upholding_Human_ Rights. pdf

Linking Artificial Intelligence Policies: http://www.linking-ai-principles.org/

OECD. (2019). Artificial Intelligence in Society. Paris: OECD Publishing. Retrieved from: https://read.oecd-ilibrary.org/science-and-technology/artificial-intelligence-insociety_eedfee77-en#page1

Politics + AI. Retrieved from: https://medium.com/politics-ai

UN ITU AI Repository. Retrieved from: https://www.itu.int/en/ITU-T/AI/Pages/ai-repository.aspx

World Economic Forum Artificial Intelligence and Machine Learning. Retrieved from: https://www.weforum.org/communities/artificial-intelligence-and-machine-learning

Index

A

Abu Bakr al-Baghdadi 33

AI and Ethics 128

AI ethics guidelines 132

Artificial Intelligence (AI) vi, 127,
128, 132, 133, 135, 137,
138, 139, 140, 142, 144,
145, 146, 148, 149, 156,
157, 187, 188, 189, 190,
191, 192, 193, 194, 195, 196

Artificial Intelligence Industry
Alliance (AIIA) 144

B

Ballistic Intelligence 6, 25

Brexit 9

British National Crime Agency
(NCA) 32

Bulk Surveillance v, 7, 38, 166

C

Chilling effects 53

Commission of Intelligence Activity 21

Communications Data 38, 39, 40,
41, 42, 43, 44, 45, 46, 47,
48, 49, 50, 51, 52, 53, 61,
62, 63, 64, 65, 66, 67, 68,
69, 70, 72, 73, 74, 76, 77,
78, 79, 83, 86, 87, 88, 91,
94, 95, 96, 100, 102, 166,
167, 168, 170, 175

Coordinated Market Economies
(CMEs) 113

Council of Europe 132, 134, 137,
166, 188

Counter-Terrorism and Border
Security Act 24

Court of Justice of the European
Union (CJEU) 40

Cyber-attacks 30, 50

D

Data Ethics Commission 138

Data protection 5

Data surveillance 38, 39, 40, 42,
44, 45, 50, 51, 53, 61, 62,
64, 65, 66, 67, 68, 73, 76,
78, 79, 83, 86, 87, 88, 91,
94, 95, 96, 100

Digital surveillance 38, 41

Donald Rumsfeld 4

Donald Trump 11

E

Edward Snowden 8

EU intelligence agencies 8, 10, 17, 18, 19

EU intelligence cooperation 15

European Commission for the Efficiency of Justice 137

European Committee on Legal Co-operation 137

European Convention on Human Rights 1, 137

European Court of Human Rights (ECHR) 2, 4, 8, 40, 45, 51, 67, 69, 72

F

Facial Recognition 3, 6, 7, 8, 198

Federal Intelligence Service 13, 19, 176, 180

G

G10 Commission 79, 80, 81, 82, 85, 96, 97, 98, 99, 100, 102, 103, 104, 177, 178

General Data Protection Regulation (GDPR) 134

German Federal Data Protection Authority (BfDI) 79

Global Positioning Satellite De-

vices 1

Grenfell Tower fire 36

Gustav Gressel 8, 159

H

Hybrid attacks 8

I

INCENSER 29

Independent Office for Police Conduct (IOPC) 26

Independent Police Complaints Commission (IPCC) 25

Intelligence and Accountability Principles 20

Intelligence and Select Committee (ISC) 18

Intelligence Surveillance i, iii, 1, 28, 57, 99, 169

Interception Communications Commissioner (IoCC) 27

Investigatory Powers Act 8, 40, 44, 49, 70, 163, 166, 167, 168, 175

Investigatory Powers Act (IPA) 8

Investigatory Powers Tribunal (IPT) 7, 29

J

John M. Nomikos 16

L

Liberal Market Economies
(LMEs) 113

M

Metadata 28, 42, 58, 66, 67, 86,
87, 102, 103, 166, 173

MI5 3, 6, 19, 32

N.

National Intelligence Priority
Framework 84

National Security Agency (NSA)
7, 29, 55

National Security Capabilities
Review (NSCR) 5

National Security Council (NSC)
11

New Irish Republican Army
(NIRA) 32

P

Pattern identification 47

Pew Research Center 55, 171

POKERFACE 29

Police Ombudsman for Northern
Ireland Policing Board
(PONIPB) 32

S

Security Sector Reforms (SSR) 26

Signals Intelligence (SIGINT) 75

Sir Kim Darroch 11

Snoopers Charter Surveillance
(SCS) 17

Strategic Defense and Security
Reviews (SDSRs) 5

Surveillance drones 58

T

Targeted surveillance 5

TEMPORA 27, 28, 29, 59, 173

U

UK's mujahedeen 33

W

WINDSTOP 29

X

XKEYSCORE 29

About the Author

Musa Khan Jalalzai is a journalist and research scholar. He has written extensively on Afghanistan, terrorism, nuclear and biological terrorism, human trafficking, drug trafficking, and intelligence research and analysis. He was an Executive Editor of the Daily Outlook Afghanistan from 2005-2011, and a permanent contributor in Pakistan's daily The Post, Daily Times, and The Nation, Weekly the Nation, (London). However, in 2004, US Library of Congress in its report for South Asia mentioned him as the biggest and prolific writer. He received Masters in English literature, Diploma in Geospatial Intelligence, University of Maryland, Washington DC, certificate in Surveillance Law from the University of Stanford, USA, and diploma in Counter terrorism from Pennsylvania State University, California, the United States.